CGP

GCSE Edexcel
Extension Science
The Workbook

This book is for anyone doing **GCSE Edexcel Extension Science**.

It's full of **tricky questions**... each one designed to make you **sweat** — because that's the only way you'll get any **better**.

There are questions to see **what facts** you know. There are questions to see how well you can **apply those facts**. And there are questions to see what you know about **how science works**.

It's also got some daft bits in to try and make the whole experience at least vaguely entertaining for you.

What CGP is all about

Our sole aim here at CGP is to produce the highest quality books — carefully written, immaculately presented and dangerously close to being funny.

Then we work our socks off to get them out to you — at the cheapest possible prices.

Contents

B3 Topic 1 — Control Systems

The Kidneys 1
More on The Kidneys 3
Reproductive Cells and The Menstrual Cycle 5
Menstrual Hormones 6
Fertility Treatments 7
X and Y Chromosomes 8
Sex-linked Genetic Disorders 9
Growth of Bacteria 10
The Immune System 11
Immunisation 12
Monoclonal Antibodies 13
More on Monoclonal Antibodies 14
Drugs From Plants and Plant Diseases 15
Daily Rhythms 16
Mixed Questions — B3 Topic 1 17

B3 Topic 2 — Behaviour and Evolution

Innate and Learned Behaviour 18
Conditioning 20
Social Behaviour and Communication 21
Animal Behaviour Studies 22
Investigating Animal Behaviour 23
Mating Behaviour 24
Parenting Behaviour 26
Plant Communication and Co-evolution 28
Fossil Evidence for Human Evolution 29
More Evidence for Human Evolution 30
Climate Change and Human Behaviour 31
Mixed Questions — B3 Topic 2 32

B3 Topic 3 — Biotechnology

Large-scale Growth of Microorganisms 33
Microorganisms and Food 35
Using Enzymes 36
Enzyme Experiments 37
Genetically Modifying Organisms 38
More on GM Organisms 39
Feeding More People 40
Biofuels 41
Mixed Questions — B3 Topic 3 42

C3a Topic 1 — Qualitative Analysis

Analysing Substances 43
Testing for Ions 44

C3a Topic 2 — Quantitative Analysis

Measuring Amounts 46
Solutions and Concentrations 47
Hard Water 48
Titrations 49
More on Titrations 50
Preparing Soluble Salts 51

C3a Topic 3 — Electrolytic Processes

Electrolysis of Molten Substances 52
Electrolysis of Solutions 53
Electrolysis Using Copper Electrodes 54
Electroplating 55
Mixed Questions — C3a Topics 1, 2 & 3 56

C3b Topic 4 — Gases, Reversible Reactions and Ammonia

Calculating Volumes 58
Reversible Reactions 59
The Haber Process 61

C3b Topic 5 — Organic Chemistry

Homologous Series.. 62
Production of Ethanol 64
Production and Issues of Ethanol 66
Ethene and Ethanoic Acid 67
Esters... 68
Uses of Esters 69
Mixed Questions — C3b Topics 4 & 5 70

P3a Topic 1 — Radiation and Treatment

Medical Physics and Ultrasound 72
Intensity of Radiation 73
Lenses.. 74
Power and the Lens Equation 77
The Eye 78
Correcting Vision Defects.. 80
Snell's Law and Total Internal Reflection 81
Uses of Total Internal Reflection................................... 82

P3a Topic 2 — X-rays and ECGs

Electron Beams.. 84
X-ray Intensity and Absorption 85
X-ray Imaging.. 86
Electricity and the Body.. 87
Pacemakers and Pulse Oximeters.................................. 88
Mixed Questions — P3a Topics 1 & 2 89

P3b Topic 3 — Radioactivity and Ionising Radiation

Particles in Atoms 92
Stability and Radioactive Decay.................................... 93
Quarks 95
Medical Uses of Radiation 96

P3b Topic 4 — Motion of Particles

Cyclotrons.. 98
Uses of Particle Accelerators 99
Momentum and Kinetic Energy.................................... 100
Annihilation and PET Scans 102

P3b Topic 5 — Kinetic Theory and Gases

Kinetic Theory and Absolute Zero................................ 103
Pressure, Volume and Temperature of Gases 104
Gas Pressure and Medicine.. 106
Mixed Questions — P3b Topics 3, 4 & 5 107

Published by CGP

Editors:
Luke Antieul, Charlotte Burrows, Emma Elder, Mary Falkner, Helena Hayes,
Felicity Inkpen, Rosie McCurrie, Hayley Thompson, Karen Wells, Sarah Williams.

Contributors:
Mike Bossart, Mike Dagless, Mark A Edwards, Max Fishel, James Foster,
Derek Harvey, Barbara Mascetti, Jim Wilson.

ISBN: 978 1 84762 857 2

With thanks to Janet Cruse-Sawyer, Catherine Davis, Chris Elliss, Murray Hamilton,
David Hickinson, Edmund Robinson and Karen Wells for the proofreading.
With thanks to Jan Greenway, Laura Jakubowski and Laura Stoney for the copyright research.

Graph to show the numbers of kidney transplant patients on page 3 reproduced with
permission from the NHS UK Transplant. www.organdonation.nhs.uk

Every effort has been made to locate copyright holders and obtain permission to reproduce
sources. For those sources where it has been difficult to trace the originator of the work, we would
be grateful for information. If any copyright holder would like us to make an amendment to the
acknowledgements, please notify us and we will gladly update the book at the next reprint.
Thank you.

Printed by Elanders Ltd, Newcastle upon Tyne.
Clipart from Corel®
Based on the classic CGP style created by Richard Parsons.

Text, design, layout and original illustrations © Coordination Group Publications Ltd. (CGP) 2011
All rights reserved.

Photocopying this book is not permitted. Extra copies are available from CGP with next day delivery.
0800 1712 712 • www.cgpbooks.co.uk

B3 Topic 1 — Control Systems

The Kidneys

Q1 One of the main roles of the **kidneys** is to remove **urea** from the blood.

a) Urea is a waste product that builds up in the blood as a result of cell metabolism. Name **one** other waste product of cell metabolism.

....

b) Tick the boxes to show whether the following statements about urea are **true** or **false**.

    True False

i) The kidneys make urea.

ii) Breaking down excess fats produces urea.

iii) The liver makes urea.

iv) The kidneys remove urea from the bloodstream.

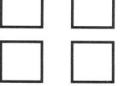

Billy the kid-ney bean

Q2 Fill in the labels on the diagram of the **urinary system** shown below. One of the labels has been done for you.

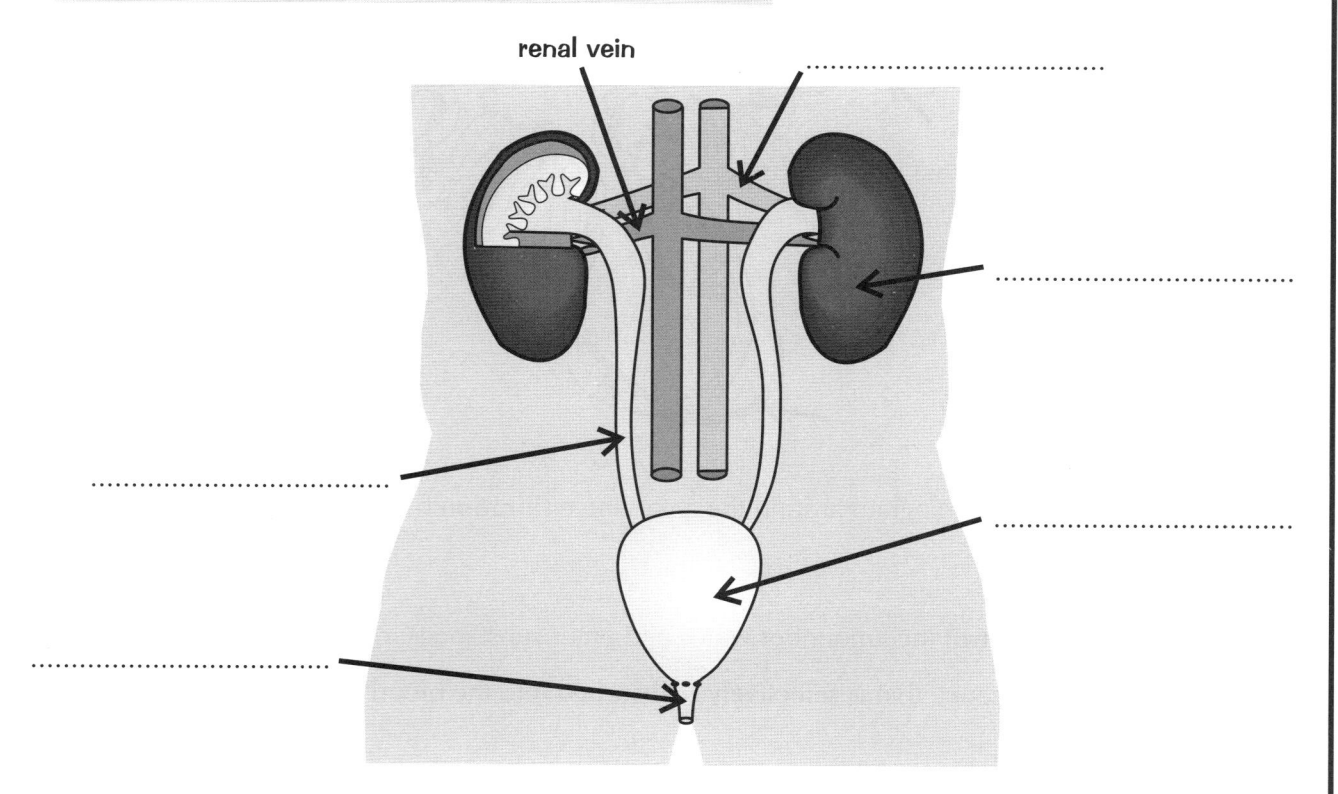

renal vein

Top Tips: Your kidneys do an ace job of filtering your blood and taking out all the stuff that you don't want or don't need any more. Without them you'd be in all sorts of trouble pretty quickly...

The Kidneys

Q3 The diagram shows the steps that occur from the **entry** to the **exit** of blood in the kidneys. Write the labels **A** to **E** in the diagram to show the correct order. The first one has been done for you.

A — Wastes, such as urea, are carried out of the nephron to the bladder.

B — A high pressure is built up which squeezes small molecules out of the blood and into the Bowman's capsule.

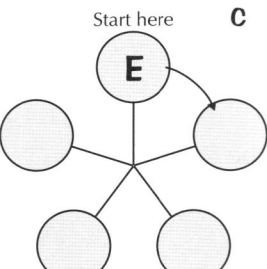

C — Useful products are reabsorbed from the nephron and enter the capillaries.

D — Molecules travel from the Bowman's capsule along the nephron.

E — Blood enters the kidney through the renal artery.

Start here: E

Q4 a) Use the words provided to fill in the missing labels on the diagram of a **nephron** shown below.

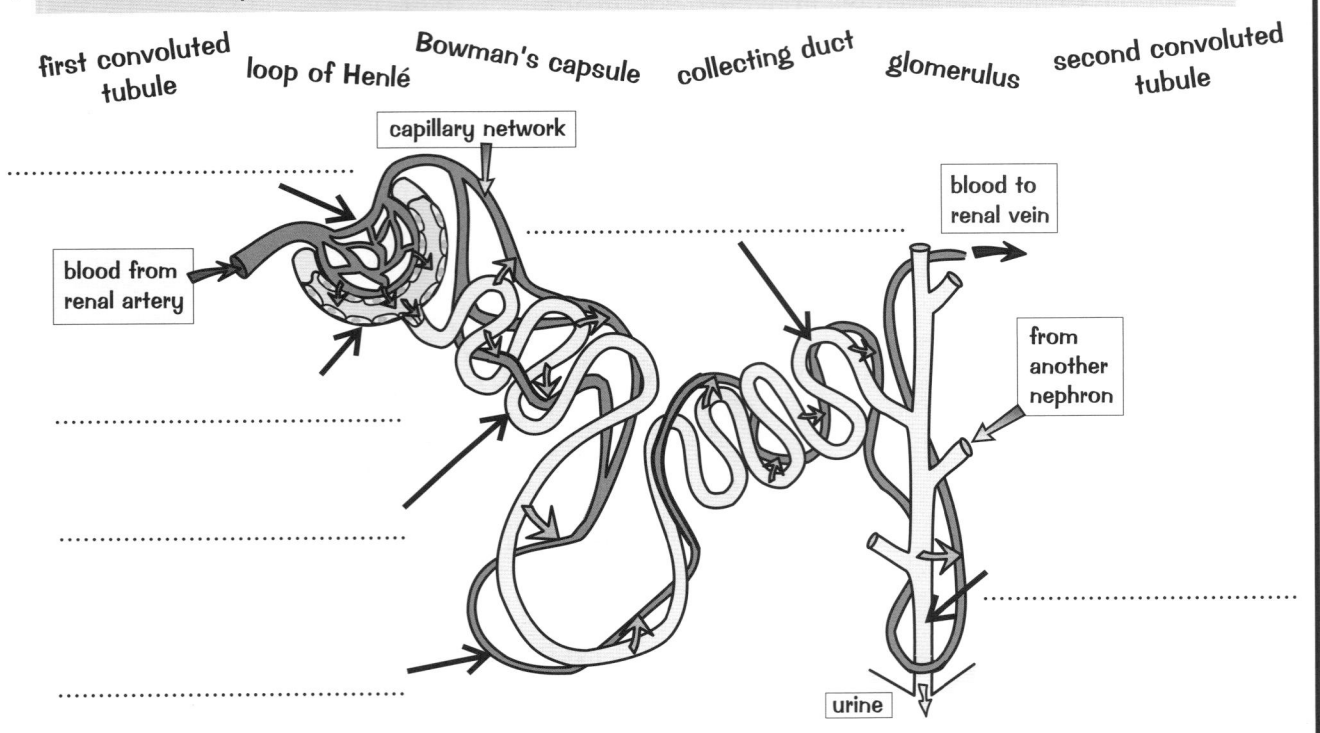

first convoluted tubule   loop of Henlé   Bowman's capsule   collecting duct   glomerulus   second convoluted tubule

b) Draw a box on the diagram around the area where **filtration** happens.

Q5 The kidneys **control** the amount of **water** and other substances in the blood.

a) Name **one** substance that is **selectively reabsorbed** into the blood by the kidneys.

....

b) The kidneys maintain the right **water content** in the body. Give the name of this process.

....

c) What is excess water removed from the body in? ....

B3 Topic 1 — Control Systems

More on The Kidneys

Q1 The concentration of water in the blood is adjusted by the **kidneys**. They ensure that the water content never gets **too high** or **too low**.

a) What is the name given to the **homeostatic mechanism** by which water content is regulated?

....

b) Complete the diagram below by circling the correct word in each pair.

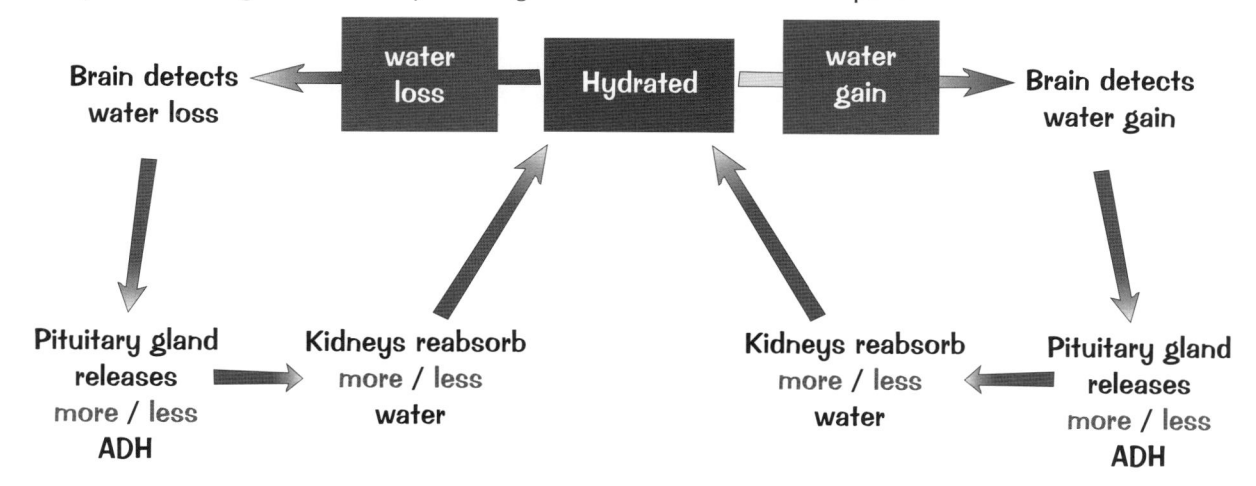

```
                    water                      water
Brain detects  ←    loss    ←  Hydrated  →    gain    →  Brain detects
water loss                                                water gain
     ↓                ↑              ↑                        ↓
Pituitary gland   Kidneys reabsorb   Kidneys reabsorb    Pituitary gland
releases          more / less        more / less         releases
more / less       water              water               more / less
ADH                                                       ADH
```

Q2 The graph shows the numbers of kidney transplant patients and numbers of donors in the **UK**.

a) i) Describe the trend in the number of people on the transplant waiting list.

....

....

....

ii) What is the general trend for donors and transplants performed compared to the number of people on the transplant waiting list?

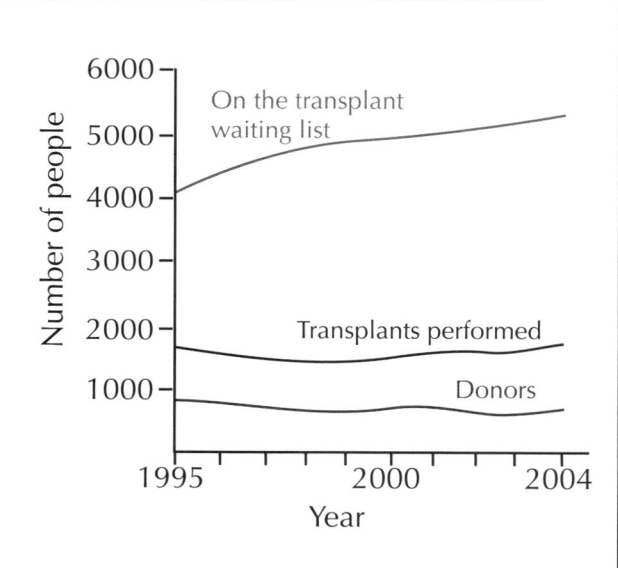

....

....

....

b) A donor kidney can be **rejected** by a patient's immune system. Suggest **one** precaution that could be taken to prevent this happening.

....

B3 Topic 1 — Control Systems

More on The Kidneys

Q3 If someone's kidneys fail they may be given a **kidney transplant** or they may have to use a **dialysis machine**. A dialysis machine does the job of the kidneys and filters the blood.

a) What substances would you expect a dialysis machine to **remove** from the blood? Tick the correct boxes.

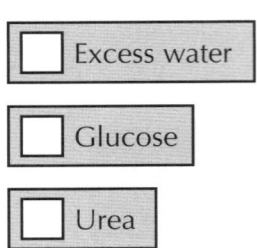

☐ Excess water

☐ Glucose

☐ Urea

The new kidney opera house was less popular than the old one.

b) Add the correct labels to the dialysis diagram.

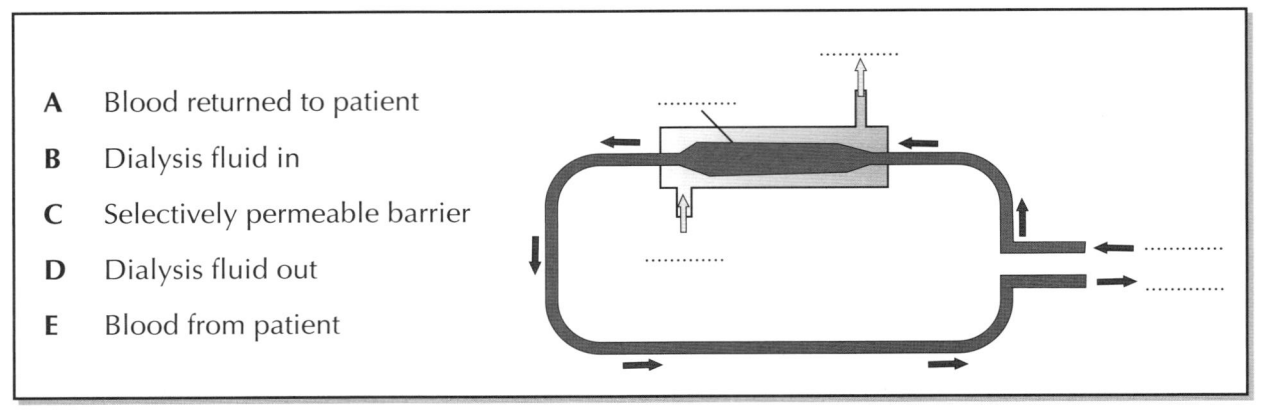

A Blood returned to patient
B Dialysis fluid in
C Selectively permeable barrier
D Dialysis fluid out
E Blood from patient

c) i) **How** does the composition of dialysis fluid compare with the composition of blood plasma?

....

ii) Why is this important?

....

d) The barrier is described as **selectively permeable**. What does this mean?

....

....

e) Explain why dialysis has to be carried out on a regular basis.

....

....

Top Tips: Dialysis is a clever technique that's saved lives. The problem is that it can take up to four hours to filter the blood and it has to be done a couple of times a week. An alternative is a kidney transplant — you can live with only one kidney, so it's possible for some people with kidney failure to receive a donated organ from a member of their family.

B3 Topic 1 — Control Systems

Reproductive Cells and The Menstrual Cycle

Q1 Below is a list of features of **reproductive cells**. Tick the boxes to show which ones are found in **sperm** and which ones are found in **eggs**.

            Sperm Eggs
a) a long tail   ☐ ☐
b) enzymes to digest cell membranes ☐ ☐
c) nutrients in cell cytoplasm to feed the embryo ☐ ☐
d) lots of mitochondria   ☐ ☐

Q2 The diagram below shows how the **uterus lining** changes during the **menstrual cycle**.

Day: 1   Day: Day: Day:

a) Fill in the missing numbers for each day. Day 1 has been done for you.

b) Fill in the remaining boxes using the labels below:

Uterus lining builds up   **Uterus lining maintained**   **Egg released (ovulation)**   **Uterus lining breaks down (menstruation)**

Q3 Sperm and eggs have **special features** to help them carry out their functions.

a) Fill in the blanks in the passage below by choosing some of the words from the box.

| head   energy   egg   sperm   oxygen   body   middle   acrosome |

A .... cell has a long tail so that it can swim to the egg. It has lots of mitochondria in its .... section to provide the .... (from respiration) needed to swim a long way. It also has an .... at the front of its 'head'. This contains the enzymes needed to digest through the membrane of an .... cell.

b) After an egg is fertilised, the structure of its cell membrane changes. Explain why this happens.

....

c) Sperm and eggs have **haploid nuclei**.

i) What is a haploid nucleus? ....

ii) Explain why both sperm and eggs have haploid nuclei.

....

B3 Topic 1 — Control Systems

Menstrual Hormones

Q1 The menstrual cycle is controlled by four hormones: **FSH**, **LH**, **progesterone** and **oestrogen**. Complete the table below to show the effects of these by placing ticks in the correct boxes.

Effect	FSH	LH	Progesterone	Oestrogen
Stimulates oestrogen production				
Inhibits FSH production				
Causes uterus lining to thicken				
Causes a follicle to mature in an ovary				
Stimulates LH surge				
Stimulates ovulation				
Maintains uterus lining				

Q2 Circle the correct word(s) from each pair to complete the paragraph below.

During the menstrual cycle, hormone levels are controlled by negative **feedback** / **feedforward**. For example, FSH stimulates the ovary to release **oestrogen** / **progesterone**. This hormone then starts to **stimulate** / **inhibit** the release of FSH from the pituitary gland. After FSH has caused a follicle to mature, negative **feedback** / **feedforward** keeps FSH levels **high** / **low** so that **no more** / **lots more** follicles mature.

Q3 If a woman becomes pregnant, her levels of **progesterone** stay high.

  a) Name the structure that secretes progesterone.
  ....

  b) Explain why a woman's level of progesterone remains high throughout pregnancy. How does this help the developing baby?
  ....
  ....
  ....

  c) Other than progesterone, the level of which hormone needs to drop for menstruation to occur?
  ....

Top Tips: Sometimes, it's haaard to be... a womaaan... Or a man for that matter, if you're trying to learn about menstrual hormones. This isn't really a topic where your natural intelligence and deep understanding of science can shine through much — you've just got to get your head down and learn what each hormone does. Sorry.

Fertility Treatments

Q1 Hormones can be used to **increase fertility**.

a) Underline **two** hormones from the list below that can be taken by a woman to increase her fertility.

FSH   oestrogen   insulin   LH   progesterone

b) Briefly explain how these hormones increase fertility.

....

c) Give **one** disadvantage of using hormones to increase fertility.

....

Q2 **Egg donation** can help a woman who can't produce eggs herself to have a child.

a) Other than being able to have a child, suggest **one** reason why a woman might choose to use donated eggs.

....

....

b) Suggest **one** disadvantage of using donated eggs to have a child.

....

Q3 *In vitro* fertilisation (**IVF**) can help couples to have children.

a) Explain how **IVF** works.

....

....

....

b) Discuss the advantages and disadvantages of IVF.

....

....

....

c) IVF can sometimes involve a **surrogate mother**.
What is a surrogate mother and when might one be used?

....

....

B3 Topic 1 — Control Systems

X and Y Chromosomes

Q1 Tick the boxes to show whether each statement is **true** or **false**.

		True	False
a)	Women have two X chromosomes. Men have an X and a Y chromosome.	☐	☐
b)	There is a 75% chance that a couple's first child will be a girl.	☐	☐
c)	Sperm cells (male gametes) can carry an X or a Y chromosome.	☐	☐
d)	If you have 4 children, you will always get 2 boys and 2 girls.	☐	☐

Q2 Here is a genetic diagram showing the inheritance of **sex chromosomes** in humans.

a) Complete the diagram to show the combinations of chromosomes in the offspring.

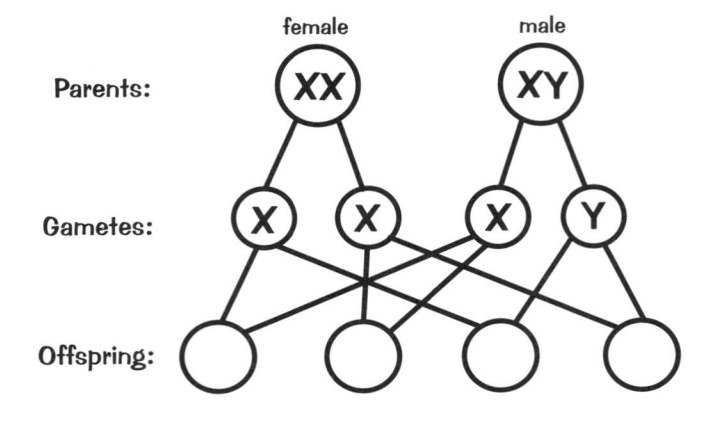

b) A woman becomes pregnant. What is the probability that the embryo is **male**?

....

Q3 **Birds** have sex chromosomes called **Z** and **W** (just like humans have X and Y). In birds, those with **two Z chromosomes** are **male**.

a) What are the female bird's sex chromosomes?

....

b) Complete the genetic diagram below to show the possible combination of gametes in bird reproduction.

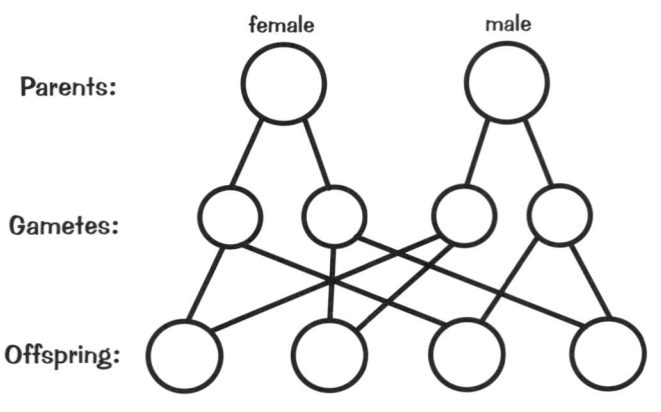

B3 Topic 1 — Control Systems

Sex-linked Genetic Disorders

Q1 **Haemophilia** is a sex-linked genetic disorder caused by a **faulty** blood clotting **allele**.

a) Explain what it means for a characteristic to be **sex-linked**.

....

b) The faulty allele is **recessive**. How many copies of the allele would the following people have:

i) a carrier .... ii) a sufferer ....

c) Complete the genetic diagram below to show the possible combinations of gametes from a **carrier** female and a **normal** (non-haemophiliac) male.

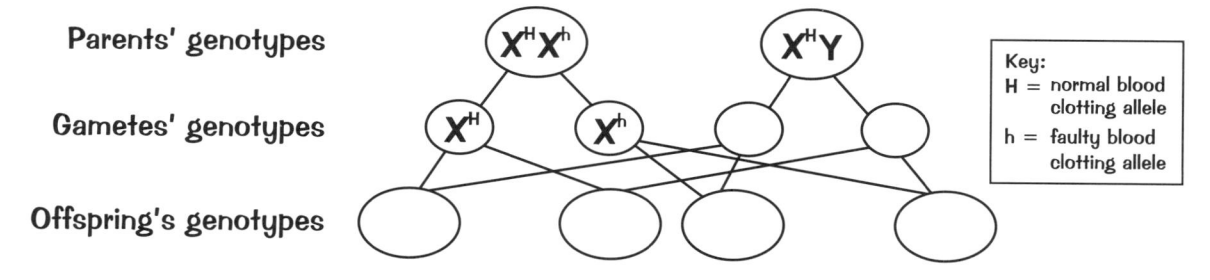

Parents' genotypes: $X^H X^h$ $X^H Y$

Gametes' genotypes: X^H X^h

Offspring's genotypes:

Key:
H = normal blood clotting allele
h = faulty blood clotting allele

d) Find the probability of their offspring having haemophilia. ....

Q2 Joe is **colour blind**. His wife Becky is a **carrier** of the faulty colour vision allele.

a) Colour blindness is a sex-linked genetic disorder. Becky draws the diagram below to show Joe all the possible combinations of alleles that their children could inherit.

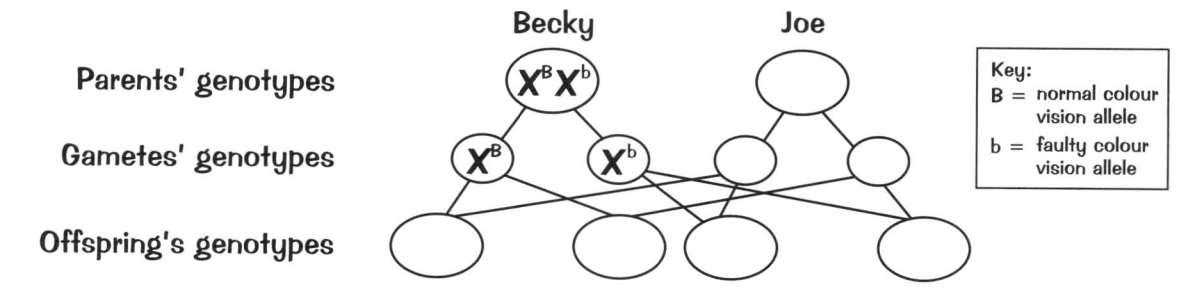

Becky   Joe

Parents' genotypes: $X^B X^b$

Gametes' genotypes: X^B X^b

Offspring's genotypes:

Key:
B = normal colour vision allele
b = faulty colour vision allele

i) What is Joe's **genotype**? ....

ii) Fill in all the empty circles to complete Becky's diagram above.

b) Joe and Becky are expecting a baby.

i) What is the probability that their baby will be colour blind? ....

ii) Joe and Becky find out they're having a baby **girl**. What is the probability that their baby girl will be colour blind? ....

Top Tips: Genetic crosses can be a bit of a faff to fill in — so take your time and work through the steps logically. After all that, you'll probably be asked to find the probability of something. Sorry.

B3 Topic 1 — Control Systems

Growth of Bacteria

Q1 Emily has a cut on her finger. **Bacteria** have got into the cut. The bacteria reproduce by **splitting into two** at regular intervals.

a) Use the axes on the right to sketch a graph showing how the population of bacteria will change over time.

b) Explain why the bacteria's ability to reproduce rapidly might be a problem for Emily.

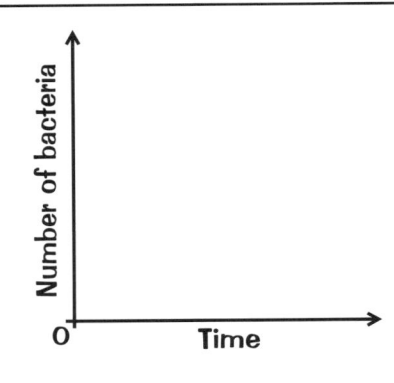

....

....

Q2 **Pasteurisation** is a process used to kill off harmful microorganisms.

a) Fill in the blanks in the passage below.

> Pasteurisation involves .... a substance, then cooling it down. This kills off most harmful microbes, so the product shouldn't make you .... Any process like this which reduces contamination by germs is called an .... technique.

Bacteria resented being put out to pasture.

b) Name the person who invented pasteurisation. ....

Q3 Dan is investigating how **temperature** affects the **growth of bacteria**. He puts **milk** into three test tubes and adds **resazurin** dye. He stores each tube at either 5 °C, 15 °C or 30 °C for 24 hours.

a) Circle the colour of resazurin dye when there's plenty of oxygen around.

    mauve   blue   colourless   lilac   pink

b) Suggest **one** thing that Dan should do to make his experiment a fair test.

....

c) The table on the right shows Dan's results after 0, 12 and 24 hours.

Time (hours)	0	12	24
Tube 1	Blue	Mauve	Colourless
Tube 2	Blue	Lilac	Mauve
Tube 3	Blue	Blue	Blue

i) Suggest which test tube Dan stored at 30 °C.

....

ii) Explain your answer to part **i**).

Remember, bacteria grow faster at higher temperatures.

....

....

B3 Topic 1 — Control Systems

The Immune System

Q1 Underline the correct description of an **antigen**.

A chemical that causes disease.   A molecule found on the surface of a microorganism.   A 'foreign' cell.   A molecule that destroys bacteria.

Q2 Myra catches **mumps**, and then she recovers. Later on she is exposed to mumps again. The graph below shows how the level of the **antibody against mumps** in Myra's blood **changes** over time.

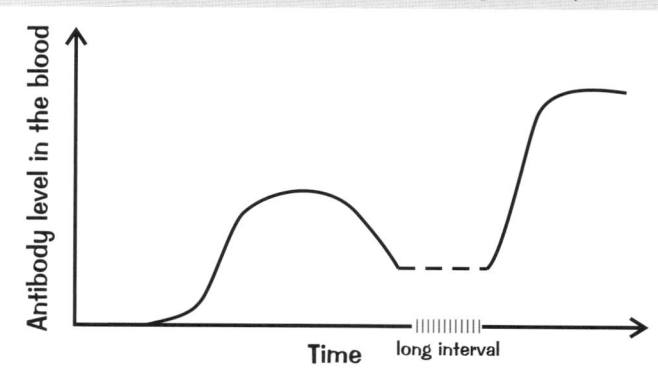

a) Write an 'X' on the graph at the point where Myra was exposed to the mumps virus for the **first** time.

b) Write a 'Y' on the graph at the point where Myra was exposed to the mumps virus for the **second** time.

c) After the first infection, Myra's body produces a special type of cell that helps her respond to the virus **faster** the second time around. Give the name of this type of cell.

....

Q3 John catches **chickenpox**. For about a week he has an itchy rash all over his skin, with a headache and a slight fever. Then the rash begins to clear up and John starts to feel better.

a) Describe how John's immune system gets rid of the chickenpox virus.

....

....

....

b) Five years later, John and his friend Jim are exposed to chickenpox at university. Jim has never had chickenpox before. Explain why Jim becomes ill, but John doesn't.

....

....

....

....

B3 Topic 1 — Control Systems

Immunisation

Q1 **Edward Jenner** invented the first vaccine, against smallpox. He came up with the idea after noticing that people who had cowpox didn't catch smallpox.

The sentences below describe the experiment that Jenner performed to test his idea. Number the sentences to show their correct order.

The first one has been done for you.

- [ ] The boy was a bit unwell, but then recovered.
- [1] Jenner took some bits of scab from a girl with cowpox.
- [ ] Jenner exposed the boy to smallpox.
- [ ] Jenner placed the bits of scab into a cut on the arm of a boy.
- [ ] The boy didn't catch smallpox.

Q2 **Immunisation** involves injecting dead or inactive microorganisms into the body.

a) Why do dead microorganisms cause the body to produce antibodies?

....

....

b) Tick the boxes to show whether the statements below about polio immunisation are **true** or **false**.

                                                                                                             True False

i) The dead or inactive polio microorganisms have some of the same antigens as the live pathogen.

ii) B-lymphocytes produce antibodies against the antigens on the injected polio microorganisms.

iii) The antigens on the dead or inactive polio microorganisms don't trigger memory lymphocytes to be made.

Q3 a) Give two **benefits** of immunisation.

1. ....

2. ....

b) Give two **risks** of immunisation.

1. ....

2. ....

B3 Topic 1 — Control Systems

Monoclonal Antibodies

Q1 The diagram on the right shows how **monoclonal antibodies** are produced in the lab.

a) Fill in the missing labels on the diagram using the words below.

tumour cells   hybridoma   antigen

monoclonal antibodies

Mouse injected with chosen ....

Fast-dividing .... from the lab

B-lymphocytes taken from mouse

The two cells are fused.

This makes a ....

It divides quickly to produce lots of ....

b) Explain why monoclonal antibodies aren't made directly from either B-lymphocytes or tumour cells.

....
....
....
....
....

Q2 Monoclonal antibodies are used in **pregnancy test sticks**. They detect a **hormone** that's found in the urine of women **only** when they are pregnant.

a) Draw lines to match the beginning of each sentence to the correct ending.

| The bit of the stick you wee on... | ...has antibodies to the hormone stuck to it (so they can't move). |

| The test strip... | ...has antibodies to the hormone, with blue beads attached. |

b) The statements below describe what happens if you **are pregnant** and you wee on the testing stick. Number them to show their correct order. The first one has been done for you.

[1] The hormone binds to the antibodies on the blue beads.

[ ] The beads and hormone bind to the antibodies on the test strip

[ ] The blue beads get stuck on the test strip, turning it blue.

[ ] The urine moves up the stick, carrying the hormone and the beads.

The test strip goes blue if you're pregnant.

c) Explain why the test strip **doesn't** turn blue if someone who is **not pregnant** wees on the stick.

....
....

Top Tips: Before some clever bods came up with the method shown above, it was really hard to make antibodies in the lab. Now they're used for all sorts of things — even sticks that you wee on...

B3 Topic 1 — Control Systems

More on Monoclonal Antibodies

Q1 Tick the boxes to show whether each statement is **true** or **false**.

a) Different cells in the body have identical antigens on their cell surface.

b) You can make monoclonal antibodies that will bind to specific cells in the body.

c) Cancer cells don't have any antigens on their cell membranes.

Q2 Monoclonal antibodies can be used to **diagnose cancer**.

a) Circle the correct word from each pair to complete the passage below.

> Antibodies that will bind to **body cells / tumour markers** are labelled with a radioactive element. The labelled antibodies are given to a patient through a drip. When the antibodies come into contact with the **body / cancer** cells, they bind to the tumour markers. A picture of the patient's body is taken using a camera that detects **radioactivity / movement**. Anywhere there are cancer cells will show up as a **dark / bright** spot.

b) Give **two** things that a doctor can tell by looking at a picture of labelled cancer cells.

....

c) Name **one** other medical problem that monoclonal antibodies can be used to diagnose.

....

Q3 Monoclonal antibodies can also be used to **treat cancer**.

a) The diagrams below show the correct order of steps in this process. Draw lines to match each label to its correct diagram.

Labels:
- The antibodies bind to the tumour markers on the cancer cells.
- An anti-cancer drug is attached to monoclonal antibodies.
- The drug kills the cancer cells but doesn't kill any normal body cells near the tumour.
- The antibodies are given to the patient through a drip.

b) Explain why it might be better for a patient to be treated with an antibody-labelled drug rather than other cancer treatments.

....

....

B3 Topic 1 — Control Systems

Drugs From Plants and Plant Diseases

Q1 Many new **drugs** that are developed are based on chemicals produced by **plants**.

a) Fill in the blanks in the passage below using the words from the box.

> pathogens   symptoms   traditional   defend   drugs
>
> Plants produce chemicals to .... themselves against pests and
> .... Some of these chemicals can be used as ....
> to treat human diseases or relieve .... A lot of our current medicines
> were discovered by studying plants used in .... cures.

b) i) Name a medical drug that humans have developed from plants. ....

   ii) What condition or symptoms is the drug you have named in part i) used to treat?

   ....

Q2 Brussel Farm grows a vegetable called **sprotilicious**. The farmers record the **crop yield** in their fields each week. The data for March is given in the table below.

Date	Sprotilicious Crop Yield (tonnes)
1st March	60
8th March	51
15th March	36
22nd March	6
29th March	0

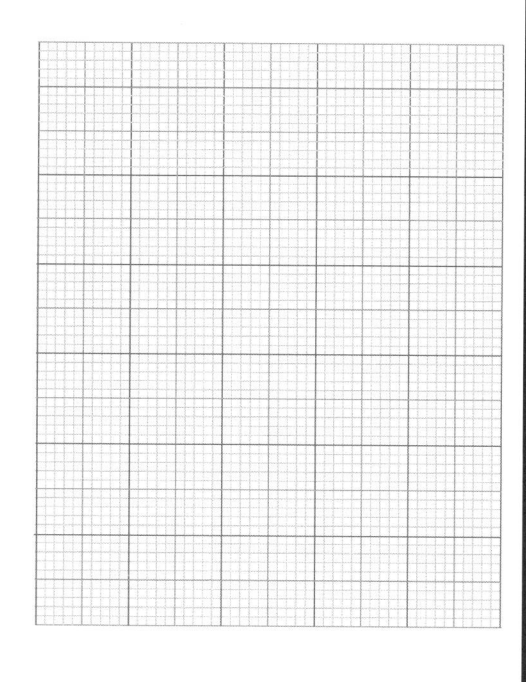

a) Draw a **bar chart** showing the change in tonnes of sprotilicious during March on the grid above.

b) i) Describe the trend shown by the graph.

   ....

   ii) Suggest what might have caused the trend shown in the graph.

   ....

   iii) What impact might the trend shown by the graph have on consumers?

   ....

B3 Topic 1 — Control Systems

Daily Rhythms

Q1 Sleep patterns are an example of a **circadian rhythm**.

a) What is a circadian rhythm?

....

b) Are circadian rhythms controlled **internally** or **externally**?

....

c) Other than sleep patterns, give **one** example of a circadian rhythm.

....

Q2 Plants show lots of different **photoperiodic responses**.

a) Tick the box next to the correct definition of a 'photoperiodic response'.

- A response to a change in the amount of light and dark in a 12 hour cycle. ☐
- A response to a change in the amount of light and dark in a 24 hour cycle. ☐
- Plant growth towards light. ☐
- Plant growth towards gravity. ☐

b) Explain why some plants:

i) only germinate when the days are very long.

....
....

ii) only flower when the day is at least a certain length.

....
....

iii) only grow when the day length is increasing.

....
....

Top Tips: Plants might look all sweet and innocent and dull, but don't let them fool you. They've got sneaky little ways of making sure they do the right stuff at the right time of the year. They're as crafty as a teacher plotting an exam revision timetable...

B3 Topic 1 — Control Systems

Mixed Questions — B3 Topic 1

Q1 Fertilisation happens when a **sperm cell** fuses with an **egg cell**. The resulting embryo grows and develops during pregnancy.

a) i) What is the probability that the embryo formed will be male? ....

ii) Circle the genotype the embryo will have if it is male.   **XX**   **XY**

b) Name the hormone that maintains the uterus lining during pregnancy. ....

c) Circle the correct word(s) from each pair to complete the paragraph below.

> Pregnancy test sticks detect a hormone found in a woman's urine only when she **is / isn't** pregnant. The test strip has **antigens / antibodies** stuck to it that can bind to this hormone. The bit you wee on contains blue beads with the same **antigens / antibodies** attached. If a woman's pregnant, the hormone binds to the **antigens / antibodies** on the blue beads. The **urine / antigen** moves up the stick, carrying the hormone and the beads. The beads and hormone bind to the antibodies on the test strip, turning it **blue / colourless**.

Q2 A **course of immunisation** against **disease B** consists of three injections at 5-week intervals, followed by a booster injection 5 years later. The graph shows the average level of antibodies in the patients' blood over the course of the programme.

a) Using the graph, explain why:

i) Three injections are needed initially.

....

....

ii) A booster injection is needed after 5 years.

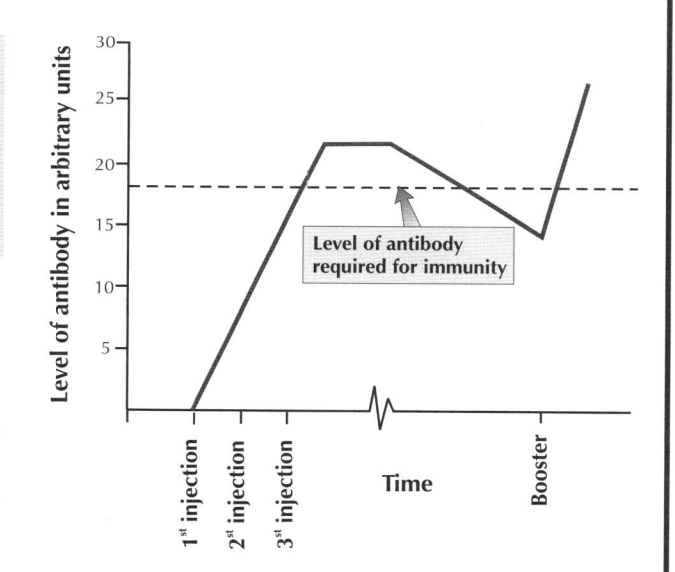

....

b) Explain how **immunisation** works.

....

....

....

B3 Topic 1 — Control Systems

B3 Topic 2 — Behaviour and Evolution

Innate and Learned Behaviour

Q1 Read the following passage and fill in the missing words, using some of the words below.

genes   environment   learned   responsive   innate

> Behaviour in animals can be inherited or ....
> — or a combination of the two. Inherited behaviour is known
> as .... behaviour. Inherited aspects of
> behaviour depend on the animal's ....

Q2 Draw lines to match up the aspects of **human behaviour** to show whether they are **innate** or **learned**.

Playing football   innate   Salivating

Sneezing   learned   Language

Q3 **Habituation** is an important part of the learning process in young animals.

a) Explain the term **habituation**.

....
....

b) Explain why habituation is **beneficial** to animals.

....

Q4 **Imprinting** is a type of behaviour seen in some animals.

a) What is **imprinting**?

....
....

b) Is imprinting a **learned behaviour**, an **innate behaviour**, or a **combination** of the two?

....

c) Name **one** type of animal that shows imprinting behaviour.

....

B3 Topic 2 — Behaviour and Evolution

Innate and Learned Behaviour

Q5 An experiment was carried out into the **feeding behaviour** of **sea anemones**. Sea anemones are simple animals that live in marine rock pools, where they are found attached to rocks. Each has a ring of **tentacles** armed with stinging cells. Anemones use the stinging cells to paralyse smaller animals swimming in the water.

Two tanks of sea water each contained a single sea anemone. The behaviour of both the sea anemones was observed for **one hour**. A volume of 'fish extract' (made by crushing some dead fish in sea water) was placed in **one** of the tanks at a certain point within the hour of observation. The number of moving tentacles for each sea anemone was recorded at five minute intervals.

Time / minutes	No. of moving tentacles	
	Tank A	Tank B
0	2	2
5	1	1
10	10	2
15	7	0
20	4	2
30	3	0
40	4	0
50	4	1
60	4	2

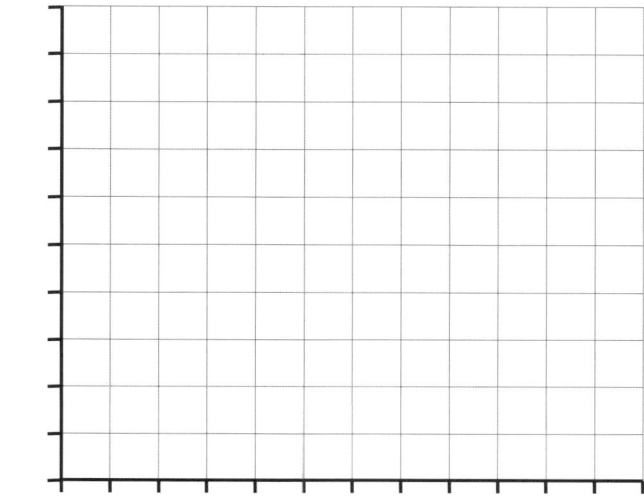

a) Draw graphs to illustrate the data on the grid provided. Use the same axes to show the results for both tanks.

b) Do you think the fish extract was added to **tank A** or to **tank B**? Explain your answer.

....

....

c) Suggest a time when the extract was added to the tank, giving a reason for your answer.

....

d) Suggest an explanation for what happened in the tank to which extract was added.

....

....

e) Do you think that this response is an example of **learned** or **innate** behaviour?

....

Top Tips: Animals are born with all the **nerve pathways** they need for **innate** behaviours **already connected**. The nerve pathways needed for **learned** behaviours develop with experience.

B3 Topic 2 — Behaviour and Evolution

Conditioning

Q1 **Conditioning** is a type of **learned behaviour**.

a) Explain the difference between '**classical** conditioning' and '**operant** conditioning'.

....

....

....

....

b) Identify each of the following examples of behaviour as either **classical conditioning** (**C**) or **operant conditioning** (**O**).

     C O

i) A baby receives food, which makes it naturally happy. It only gets food when its mother is present. When its mother is present it feels happiness. ☐ ☐

ii) A rat is provided with a maze, at the end of which is a food reward. After many trials, the rat learns to complete the maze and reach the reward without error. ☐ ☐

iii) A child learns how to ride a bike. ☐ ☐

iv) A dolphin learns to associate being given food with its trainer blowing a whistle. ☐ ☐

Q2 **Police sniffer dogs** undergo a period of intensive training. This involves teaching the dogs to **find illegal substances**, like drugs, and **alert their handlers** to what they've found.

a) Suggest **one** form of **operant conditioning** that could be used to encourage a dog to find an illegal substance and then alert their handler.

....

b) Give **one** other example of operant conditioning being used to train animals in the police force.

....

Q3 Describe **one** example of when classical conditioning is used **in combination** with operant conditioning when training captive animals.

....

....

....

....

B3 Topic 2 — Behaviour and Evolution

Social Behaviour and Communication

Q1 List three reasons why animals **communicate** with one another.

1. ....
2. ....
3. ....

Q2 Below is a list of different **types** of communication used by different kinds of animals. In each case, suggest a **reason** for the communication.

a) A peacock raises and shakes its long coloured tail feathers.

....

b) A butterfly flashes its wings to show spots that look like large, staring eyes.

....

c) A honey bee does a 'waggle dance' in the hive.

....

d) A dog rolls onto its back.

....

Q3 Some animals use **pheromones** to communicate.

a) What is a pheromone?

....

b) Suggest why a female moth might release a pheromone into the air.

....

Q4 The **chiffchaff** and the **willow warbler** are two related species of woodland birds. They are both green-brown in colour and spend much of their time among the foliage of trees.

Suggest why these birds attract mates using song rather than visual signals.

....
....

B3 Topic 2 — Behaviour and Evolution

Animal Behaviour Studies

Q1 Draw lines to match the ethologist to their research.

Jane Goodall	Imprinting in geese.
Nikolaas Tinbergen	Social behaviour in gorillas.
Dian Fossey	Social behaviour in chimpanzees.
Konrad Lorenz	Innate behaviour in gulls.

Q2 Describe how **imprinting** is a beneficial behaviour for goose chicks.

....

Q3 Give **two** examples of social behaviour in gorillas and chimpanzees.

1. ....

2. ....

Q4 Experiments were carried out to investigate feeding behaviour in young **herring gulls**. The young peck at the bill of the parent to stimulate it to regurgitate fish, which the young then swallow. This behaviour occurs soon after the young hatch. Scientists presented young herring gulls with a series of **cardboard models** of a parent gull's head. The results of the study are shown below. Real adult herring gulls have a **white head**, with a **yellow bill** and a **red spot** near the tip.

Model	White head, grey bill, no spot	White head, grey bill, red spot	White head, yellow bill, red spot	Pointed red stick with three white bands
No. of pecks by young	5	39	42	50

a) Describe what these experiments demonstrate about what stimulates feeding behaviour in young herring gulls. Explain your answer.

....

....

....

b) Is this behaviour innate or learned? Give a reason for your answer.

....

B3 Topic 2 — Behaviour and Evolution

Investigating Animal Behaviour

Q1 Tick the correct box to show whether each of the statements below is **true** or **false**.

		True	False
a)	A choice chamber is a container with one big chamber in the middle.	☐	☐
b)	Choice chambers are often used to investigate the behaviour of insects.	☐	☐
c)	In a choice chamber, an animal will usually head to environmental conditions that are closest to their natural habitat.	☐	☐
d)	You can use choice chambers to investigate how animals respond to genetic factors.	☐	☐
e)	Once an animal goes into one of the chambers they can't get out again.	☐	☐

Q2 Jerry wanted to investigate woodlice behaviour. He set up a **choice chamber** with four different sections, as shown on the right. He put **10 woodlice** into the centre and then put the lid on. After 15 minutes, he recorded the number of woodlice in each chamber. His results are shown in the table.

Chamber	1	2	3	4
No. of woodlice	7	2	1	0

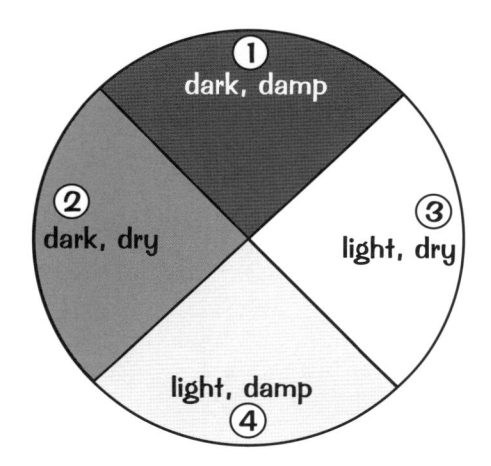

Choice chamber sections:
① dark, damp
② dark, dry
③ light, dry
④ light, damp

a) Suggest why Jerry put all the woodlice into the centre of the choice chamber at the beginning of the experiment.

....

b) i) Describe what the results show about the conditions woodlice prefer.

....

....

....

ii) Suggest why the woodlice prefer these conditions in the choice chamber.

....

....

c) Give **two** conditions that Jerry should have controlled in his experiment to make it a fair test.

1. ....

2. ....

B3 Topic 2 — Behaviour and Evolution

Mating Behaviour

Q1 Different **species** can have very different **mating strategies**.

Circle the correct word from each pair to complete these sentences about mating behaviour.

a) **Monogamy / Courtship** means staying with just one mate for life.
It's pretty **common / rare** in the animal kingdom.

b) In many species one **male / female** will mate with several **males / females** during one breeding season.

c) In some mammals, one male has a group of females and mates with **all / none** of them, e.g. **gibbons / lions**.

Q2 **Swans** mate for life — once a pair have mated, they only breed with each other. Explain why this behaviour is unusual, and describe some more common mating patterns.

....
....
....

Q3 **Male frigate birds** have red sacs on their chests. During the mating season, males **display** by inflating this sac, as shown in the picture.

a) What type of behaviour is this?

....

b) What advantage might the male frigate bird gain from this behaviour?

....
....

c) In most bird species the female is **duller** in appearance than the male. Explain why this is.

....
....
....

B3 Topic 2 — Behaviour and Evolution

Mating Behaviour

Q4 In most species, **males compete** to win the right to mate with females. Methods used vary from bringing the female gifts of food to fighting off the other males. However, it is the **opposite** way around in **seahorses** — females compete for the attention of males. Seahorses are also unusual in that the female lays her eggs in the male's pouch and **he** is then '**pregnant**' with the young and eventually gives birth to them.

a) Explain fully why males usually compete for females, and suggest why this is not the case in seahorses.

....

....

....

....

....

b) Why is it important for most animals that females don't mate with a male of a closely related species?

....

....

Q5 Male **crickets** and **grasshoppers** attract females by a process called '**stridulation**', where they rub rough parts of their body together. Crickets rub their wings together and grasshoppers rub their legs over their wings. The result is a **chirping sound**.

a) Different species of crickets and grasshoppers produce different patterns of chirps, in terms of volume, pitch and frequency of chirps. Suggest why.

....

b) The 'songs' of different species of grasshopper are more distinctive than the songs of different species of cricket. What does this suggest about the **appearance** of different species of the two kinds of insects. Explain your answer.

....

....

....

Top Tips: The male **bowerbird** impresses females by constructing an elaborate mound of earth decorated lavishly with shells, leaves, feathers and flowers, which he spends **hours** carefully arranging.

B3 Topic 2 — Behaviour and Evolution

Parenting Behaviour

Q1 In many species of **birds**, **both** parents play a role in incubating eggs and feeding the young once the eggs have hatched.

a) State an advantage of this shared responsibility for:

i) the young. ....

....

ii) the parents. ....

....

b) **Birds of paradise** differ in that the females have sole responsibility for looking after the young. These birds live on the island of New Guinea, where there are few predators.

Suggest a possible link between the reproductive behaviour of birds of paradise and the fact that there are few predators in their habitat.

....

....

....

Q2 Some animals **care for their young** for long periods, while others provide **no parental care** at all.

a) Give **three** ways in which animals may care for their young.

1. ....

2. ....

3. ....

b) Explain how caring for their young may put the parents at **risk**.

Think about how doing the things you listed in part a) might cause problems for the parents.

....

....

....

Q3 Explain why parental care can be a **successful evolutionary strategy**.

....

....

B3 Topic 2 — Behaviour and Evolution

Parenting Behaviour

Q4 The table compares the **average number of offspring** produced per female per year for some different animal species.

Species	Average number of offspring per year
Orang-utan	0.25
Wood mouse	20
Sperm whale	0.1
Red fox	5
Green turtle	200

a) Explain how it is possible for the average number of offspring per year of the orang-utan and the sperm whale to be less than one.

....

....

b) On average, a female wood mouse gives birth to **five** offspring after a pregnancy. Explain how 20 offspring can be produced per year.

....

c) Which species of animal is likely to show the least degree of parental care? Give a full explanation for your answer.

....

....

....

....

d) Which species of animal is likely to have the greatest proportion of their young survive? Explain your answer.

....

....

....

Top Tips: Ah, parents — we'd be stuffed without them. We'd have no-one to make our tea, do our ironing or mop our sweaty brows when we were sick. But worst of all we'd have no-one's bank balance to drain. And all we have to do is put up with a bit of nagging. Seems fair to me.

B3 Topic 2 — Behaviour and Evolution

Plant Communication and Co-evolution

Q1 Use the words provided to complete the paragraph below about how insects help to **pollinate** plants.

| plants | nectar | pollen | chemicals |

Lots of flowers are scented — they release smelly .... to attract insects. The insects come to the flower looking for sugary .... While they're there, some .... gets stuck to them. When they fly away, they carry it with them and pass it on to other ....

Q2 When some plants are **eaten by insect pests** they release **chemicals**.

a) Some of these chemicals attract **insect predators**. Explain how these predators help the plant.

....

b) Plants can also communicate with **nearby plants** using the chemicals they release. Explain how this helps the nearby plants.

....

....

Q3 The **button-plant** produces chemicals in its nectar which kill insects that try to eat it. But Professor Route has discovered a species of **butterfly** that **can** eat the nectar. She thinks the button-plant and the butterfly might have **co-evolved**.

a) What is co-evolution?

....

b) Do you think the button-plant and the butterfly co-evolved? Explain your answer.

....

....

....

....

Mmm, tasty.

B3 Topic 2 — Behaviour and Evolution

Fossil Evidence for Human Evolution

Q1 Draw lines to connect each fossil or group of fossils to the correct **age**.

Ardi	3.2 million years old
Lucy	1.6 million years old
Hominids discovered by Leaky	4.4 million years old

Q2 Circle the correct word in each pair to complete the sentences about **Ardi** below.

a) Ardi had **long / short** arms and **long / short** legs — more like an ape than a human.

b) She had an **ape-like / human-like** toe.

c) Her brain was about the same size as a **chimpanzee / human**.

d) The structure of Ardi's legs suggests she walked like a **chimpanzee / human**.

e) Her hand bones suggest that she **did / didn't** use her hands to help her walk.

Q3 Use the words provided to complete the paragraph below.

You can use each word once, more than once, or not at all.

| smaller | human | short | larger | walking upright | climbing trees | ape | long |

Turkana-boy, a fossil discovered by Leakey, is more like a .... than Lucy. His .... arms and .... legs are much more like a .... than an .... His brain size was much .... than Lucy's. The structure of his legs and feet suggests he was better adapted to ....

Q4 **Lucy** is a fossil hominid who was found in Ethiopia.

a) Is Lucy **more** or **less** human-like than the fossil Ardi?

....

b) Explain your answer to part **a)**.

....

....

....

B3 Topic 2 — Behaviour and Evolution

More Evidence for Human Evolution

Q1 Studying **mitochondrial DNA** can help us to understand how humans have **evolved**.

a) Tick the correct boxes to show whether the statements below are **true** or **false**.

	True	False
i) You inherit all of your mitochondrial DNA from your father.	☐	☐
ii) Everyone on the planet has similar mitochondrial DNA.	☐	☐
iii) Studying mitochondrial DNA has shown that everyone is descended from one woman — 'Mitochondrial Eve'.	☐	☐

b) Choose words from the box to fill in the gaps in the passage below.

high	evolved	migrated	200 000	Africa	mutations

Some bits of mitochondrial DNA vary from person to person due to ....
Mitochondrial DNA has a .... mutation rate. Scientists studying
the changes in mitochondrial DNA have worked out that 'Mitochondrial Eve' lived in
.... about .... years ago. This means that
Homo sapiens must have .... there, and then ....
to other areas of the world.

Mitochondrial Eve is also known as African Eve.

Q2 The **stone tools** shown on the right are part of a museum display about **human evolution**.

a) i) Circle the tool that you think was made **most recently**.

ii) Explain your answer to part i).

....

....

....

Tool A   **Tool B**

b) The label in the museum next to Tool B says that it is approximately 200 000 years old. Describe **one** way that scientists might have worked out how old it is.

....

....

Q3 Both **mitochondrial DNA** and **nuclear DNA** can be used to study **human evolution**.

Give **two** reasons why mitochondrial DNA can be more useful for this than nuclear DNA.

1. ....

2. ....

B3 Topic 2 — Behaviour and Evolution

Climate Change and Human Behaviour

Q1 Humans lived through the last **ice age**, which brought about a change in temperature and food that was available to eat. As their **environment changed**, humans **changed their behaviour** so that they could survive in the new environment.

    a) What is an ice age?

    ....

    ....

    b) Suggest how humans changed their behaviour to cope with:

        i) the change in temperature.

        ....

        ....

        ii) the change in food availability.

        ....

        ....

Q2 When humans **migrated** out of Africa they found lots of **new environments**. For example, in Europe they found a new range of plants, much larger animals, and that it was much colder.

    a) Suggest how the behaviour of humans changed when they arrived in Europe.

    ....

    ....

    ....

    b) **i)** Give another example of an area that humans migrated to from Africa.

        ....

        ii) Give **one** change that occurred in their behaviour when humans migrated to the area you named in part **i)**.

*Think about how the place you named would be **different** to what they were used to before.*

        ....

        ....

Top Tips: The last **real** ice age ended more than 10 000 years ago — but we've had some cold blips since then. For example, things got a bit chilly between the 16th and 19th centuries — it was so cold in winter that the Thames used to freeze and people held a fair on the ice. Brrrr.

B3 Topic 2 — Behaviour and Evolution

Mixed Questions — B3 Topic 2

Q1 Many people keep **dogs** either as **companions** or as **working** animals.
The domesticated dog is similar in many ways to **wild dogs** which live in parts of Africa.

a) A domesticated dog can be taught to 'sit' by rewarding it every time it responds correctly to the 'sit' command. What type of conditioning is this an example of? Underline the correct answer.

          classical   operant

b) Many domesticated dogs are useful as guards, because they will bark loudly if they hear a burglar breaking into the house, but don't bark at noises from people or cars just passing the house.

Suggest why dogs respond to the quiet noise of a burglar but not to the louder noise from cars.

....

....

c) Dogs often communicate with other dogs using chemicals, for example to mark their territories. What are these chemicals called?

....

d) Both wild dogs and domesticated dogs feed their young on milk for several weeks after birth. How does a newborn puppy 'know' to suckle from its mother?

....

e) After birth, young wild dogs spend several months with their parents, who protect them from predators and teach them to hunt effectively.

   i) Outline the possible **disadvantages** for the parents of this behaviour.

....

   ii) Explain why this behaviour is a **good evolutionary strategy**, despite its disadvantages.

....

....

Q2 Most **birds** reproduce by laying a **small** clutch of eggs, and keeping them warm until they hatch into **chicks**. They then tend the chicks in the nest for several weeks.

a) **Frogs** lay **large** clumps of frogspawn in a pond and then leave — they don't tend the spawn or the tadpoles which hatch from it. Explain why frogs don't need to look after their young but birds do.

....

....

b) The 'cheeping' of a young bird stimulates its parent to feed it. Give two other 'uses' of bird calls.

....

B3 Topic 2 — Behaviour and Evolution

B3 Topic 3 — Biotechnology

Large-scale Growth of Microorganisms

Q1 Complete the passage about **biotechnology** by filling in the gaps using the words below.

| dead | microorganisms | mammals | useful | services | living |

Biotechnology means using .... organisms, especially

...................., to produce .... products

(e.g. food or medicines) or to provide people with ....

(e.g. waste management or water purification).

Q2 The diagram on the right shows a **fermenter**.

a) What is a fermenter?

....

....

....

b) Why is it important for a fermenter to have the right conditions?

....

....

....

Think about the conditions microorganisms need to grow to help you answer part c).

c) Explain the purpose of each of the following:

i) the water jacket

....

ii) the air supply

....

iii) the paddles

....

d) Explain why aseptic conditions are needed in the fermenter.

....

Large-scale Growth of Microorganisms

Q3 The diagram on the right shows an experiment to investigate the effects of different factors on **yeast growth** under **anaerobic conditions**.

a) Describe the changes you would expect to see in the lime water and explain why.

....

....

b) Suggest **one** way you could measure the yeast's **rate of respiration**.

....

....

c) Give **two** factors that are likely to affect the respiration rate of yeast.

1. ....

2. ....

Q4 A group of students set up the experiment below to simulate the conditions in a **fermenter**.

1. Make up the culture medium and put it into a sterile flask.
2. Add a sample of the microorganism (yeast).
3. Seal the flask with a ventilated bung that lets gas out but not in.
4. Mix thoroughly then place in the incubator at 37 °C.
5. Remove from the incubator for mixing every 15 minutes.

a) George set up his experiment but forgot to put the flask into the incubator. Suggest what effect this would have on his experiment.

....

b) The teacher asked pupils to take a small sample of their culture medium and test it with Universal Indicator paper. Why did they need to do this?

....

c) Do you think that the yeast cells were respiring aerobically or anaerobically? Explain your answer.

....

B3 Topic 3 — Biotechnology

Microorganisms and Food

Q1 Complete the passage about **yoghurt making** by filling in the gaps using the words below.

> fermenter   cooled   lactose   ferment   clot
> pasteurised   lactic acid   bacteria   incubated

To make yoghurt, milk is .... to kill off any unwanted microorganisms, then .... Next, a starter culture of .... is added and the mixture is .... in a .... The bacteria .... the .... sugar in the milk to form .... This causes the milk to .... and form yoghurt.

Q2 **Mycoprotein** is a food source that comes from fungi.

a) What is mycoprotein used to replace in food?

....

b) Give **one** advantage of using mycoprotein as a food source.

....

c) Name the fungus that mycoprotein is made from.

....

Q3 Give three advantages of producing **foods** using **microorganisms** rather than other organisms.

1. ....

2. ....

3. ....

Q4 Yoghurt is made by fermenting milk. **Yoghurt production** can be affected by different factors.

a) Explain why the **pH** of milk **decreases** as yoghurt is produced.

....

b) For **one** named factor, describe its effect on the rate of yoghurt production.

....

....

B3 Topic 3 — Biotechnology

Using Enzymes

Q1 The Complacent Cow Company makes **cheese** from cow's milk using an **enzyme** that comes from **genetically modified yeast**. They claim that they "make cheese without cruelty to animals".

a) Name the enzyme that the Complacent Cow Company uses.

....

b) Describe briefly how yeasts can be made to produce this enzyme.

....

c) Suggest why the Complacent Cow Company's cheese might be popular with vegetarians, but cheese from other companies might not be.

....

....

Q2 A sweet manufacturer uses an enzyme produced by **yeast** to convert **sucrose** into **fructose**.

a) Name the enzyme involved in this process.

....

b) Name the **yeast** that naturally produces this enzyme.

....

c) Explain the purpose of converting sucrose into fructose.

....

....

Q3 **Bacteria** produce enzymes to help break down their food. One example is the **protease enzyme**, which breaks down **protein** into amino acids.

Some **washing powders** have the protease added to them. Explain why.

....

....

....

Top Tips: Phew — bet you never thought there were so many useful little enzymes out there. Well, there's a shed load, but luckily you only need to know about a couple. Make sure you remember what they are for the exam — it could pick you up some marks, and it'll even impress your mates.

B3 Topic 3 — Biotechnology

Enzyme Experiments

Q1 Enzymes can be **immobilised** using various methods.

a) Give **one** way that enzymes can be immobilised.

....

b) Suggest **one** benefit of using immobilised enzymes.

....

Q2 Some kinds of **dairy product** are treated to remove the **lactose** (milk sugar).

a) Suggest why this is done.

....

b) Briefly describe how immobilised enzymes are used to produce lactose-free milk.

....

....

c) Suggest how you could test whether the milk produced is definitely lactose-free.

....

....

Q3 **Pectinases** are enzymes that break down pectin in the cell walls of plants. Aslan does an experiment to see how **pectinase** activity varies with **pH**. He adds pectinase to crushed apples at different pH values to release their juice. The graph shows his results.

a) Suggest why the fruit is crushed before pectinase is added.

....

....

b) What is the optimum pH for the activity of this pectinase?

....

c) Suggest **one** factor that Aslan needs to keep the same during this experiment.

....

d) Some types of fruit, such as oranges, are more acidic than apples. A different kind of pectinase is needed to get juice from oranges effectively. Suggest how the graph above would be different for a pectinase that works well at extracting juice from oranges.

....

B3 Topic 3 — Biotechnology

Genetically Modifying Organisms

Q1 Some stages in the production of a **herbicide-resistant maize plant** are listed below. Put the stages in the correct order.

A The herbicide-resistance gene is inserted into *Agrobacterium tumefaciens*.

B Infected cells from maize are grown in a medium containing herbicide.

C The gene that makes a wild corn plant resistant to herbicide is identified.

D *Agrobacterium tumefaciens* is allowed to infect a maize plant.

E The herbicide-resistance gene is cut out from a wild corn plant.

Order: ....

Q2 a) Match the descriptions below to the different stages of **insulin production** by putting the correct letter next to the diagram.

A Insulin produced by the bacteria is purified and can then be used as a treatment.

B The plasmid is put back into the bacteria and they are cultivated until millions of identical bacteria have grown.

C An enzyme cuts the plasmid so that the human section of DNA can be inserted.

D A human DNA sample is taken and a plasmid (bacterial DNA) is removed from the bacteria.

E Enzymes are used to cut the human insulin gene from the human DNA.

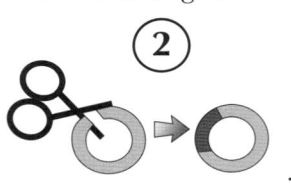

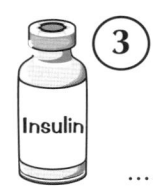

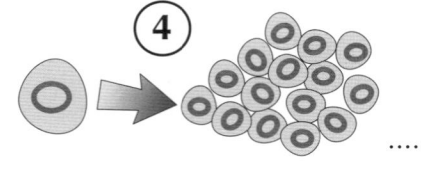

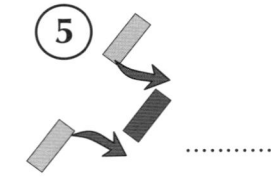

b) Arrange the numbers to give the steps in the correct order. ....

c) i) Describe the role of **restriction enzymes** in the production of insulin.

....

ii) The restriction enzymes leave DNA with 'sticky ends'. What are **sticky ends**?

....

d) Briefly describe the role of **ligase** in insulin production.

....

B3 Topic 3 — Biotechnology

More on GM Organisms

Q1 Tick the correct box to show whether the statements below are **true** or **false**.

		True	False
a)	Developed countries don't have any health problems.	☐	☐
b)	Tomatoes have been genetically engineered to have 'anti-cancer' properties.	☐	☐
c)	Purple tomatoes have been developed as an easy way to get protein into people's diets.	☐	☐
d)	Flavonoids are molecules that are thought to protect against cancers and heart disease.	☐	☐
e)	Scientists have genetically engineered tomatoes that contain the flavonoid gene.	☐	☐

Q2 a) Use the words provided to fill in the blanks in the passage below.

harmful   kills   bacterium   gene   resistant   cotton

> *Bacillus thuringiensis* (Bt) is a .... that can be used in biotechnology. It produces a toxin that .... many of the insect larvae that are .... to crops. The .... for this toxin can be inserted into crops like .... These crops then produce the toxin in their stems and leaves, making them .... to the insect pests.

b) Give **one disadvantage** of using crops that produce Bt toxin rather than normal crops.

....

Q3 Unicourt Biotech, an American company, has developed a new **GM rice** that gives a **higher yield** than ordinary rice and which is also **resistant to diseases**.

Ruritasia is a poor island in South-East Asia. The rice would grow well there, but some of the local farmers **don't** want to use it.

a) Why might it be good for the people of Ruritasia if they used the GM rice?

....

....

b) Some people in Ruritasia object to the use of GM rice. Suggest one objection they might have.

....

c) If the climate in Ruritasia changed, resulting in lack of rain, what kind of GM crop could be used?

....

B3 Topic 3 — Biotechnology

Feeding More People

Q1 Use the words provided to fill in the blanks in the passage below.

> food security   increase   production   rising   nutrition   amount

The world's population is .... very quickly, which means that global food .... must .... too. This is so that we all have enough food to eat with the right balance of .... — this is known as .... We also need to make sure that people still have the same .... of food to eat.

Q2 Some farmers try to reduce the number of **pests** on their crops.

a) Why is it beneficial for farmers to reduce pest numbers?

....

b) Suggest **two** ways in which a farmer can reduce pest numbers.

1. ....

2. ....

Q3 There are two varieties of **wheat plants** that have the characteristics outlined below:

WHEAT PLANT	GRAIN YIELD	RESISTANCE TO BAD WEATHER
Tall plant	High	Low
Dwarf plant	Low	High

a) Describe how selective breeding could be used to create a wheat plant with a **high yield** and **high resistance** to bad weather.

....

....

....

b) Other than selective breeding or managing pests, give **one** way a farmer could increase crop yield.

....

B3 Topic 3 — Biotechnology

Biofuels

Q1 Tick the box next to the correct definition of **biofuels**.

- Fuels made from plants, animals or their waste products. ☐
- Fuels that have been made through genetic engineering. ☐
- Fuels that are made from animals only. ☐
- Fuels that power biological technologies. ☐

Q2 Overall, **biofuels** don't release as much **carbon dioxide** into the atmosphere as fossil fuels. Explain why this is.

....

....

....

Q3 **Biofuels** are a **renewable** source of fuel and can be used instead of fossil fuels.

a) i) Why are biofuels considered to be **renewable**?

....

ii) Give an **advantage** of renewable fuels over fossil fuels.

....

b) One **disadvantage** of using biofuels is that growing the crops needed to make them take up a large amount of land. Explain why this is could be a problem.

....

....

c) Suggest **another disadvantage** of using biofuels.

....

Top Tips:
The simple fact is that fossil fuels aren't great for the environment and they're running out — so we need an alternative. Biofuels are pretty handy, but don't be fooled into thinking they're the perfect solution. They've got disadvantages too, so make sure you know the pros AND cons.

B3 Topic 3 — Biotechnology

Mixed Questions — B3 Topic 3

Q1 Circle the correct word in each pair to complete the sentences below about **food production**.

a) Global food production needs to **increase** / **decrease** so that we all have **food** / **job** security.

b) Crop yield can be improved by genetically engineering plants that are **waterproof** / **resistant** to **pests** / **biogas**.

c) Crop yield can also be improved by selecting and breeding plants with the **best** / **worst** characteristics over several generations, to develop desired **enzymes** / **traits**.

d) Food crops can be **pasteurised** / **genetically engineered** to increase their yield, e.g. by producing **insect-resistant** / **blue-eared** crops.

Q2 The statements below are about **enzymes** that are used in biotechnology. Tick the correct box to show whether each statement is **true** or **false**.

True False

a) Biological washing powders don't contain enzymes. ☐ ☐

b) *Fusarium* is an enzyme that breaks down food. ☐ ☐

c) A bacterium called *Saccharomyces cerevisiae* produces invertase. ☐ ☐

d) Invertase is an enzyme that converts glucose into sucrose. ☐ ☐

e) Chymosin is used in the process of making vegetarian cheese. ☐ ☐

f) You can use immobilised lactase to produce lactose-free milk. ☐ ☐

g) Immobilised enzymes are enzymes that don't work. ☐ ☐

h) Ligase is an enzyme involved in insulin production. ☐ ☐

Q3 Charlotte works for a company that uses **microorganisms** to produce their products.

a) How are microorganisms grown on a **large scale**?

....

b) Suggest **one** product that Charlotte's company could manufacture using **bacteria**.

....

c) i) Name one other type of microorganism that humans can obtain useful products from.

....

ii) Name **one** product that can be made from the type of microorganism you named in part **i)**.

....

B3 Topic 3 — Biotechnology

Analysing Substances

Q1 Use the words to complete the passage.

| much | only | quantitative | sample | qualitative |

The first stage in any analysis is to choose the most suitable analytical method. A .... method can be used if you .... want to find out what substances are present in a ...., but if you want to find out how .... of each substance is present then a .... analysis is necessary.

Q2 Give **two situations** where analytical techniques are used.

1. ....

2. ....

Q3 Maria was asked to identify the **solute** present in a sample of water. It was known to be a single ionic compound.

> Step 1 — Maria took 5 cm³ of the water and added a small quantity of sodium hydroxide solution. A **white precipitate** was formed that dissolved when more of the alkali was added. This told Maria that the **aluminium ion** was present.
>
> Step 2 — Maria took a further 25 cm³ of water and added some dilute hydrochloric acid followed by an excess of barium chloride solution. A **white precipitate** was formed showing Maria that the **sulfate ion** was present.

a) Explain why the test for an ion must be unique.

....

b) Circle the correct answer for each of the following questions.

   i) What sort of analysis is carried out in Step 1 of the procedure? **qualitative / quantitative**

   ii) What sort of analysis is carried out in Step 2 of the procedure? **qualitative / quantitative**

c) What must be the identity of the mystery solute? ....

Top Tips: Chemical analysis is vital — chemists often need to know what's in a substance. Make sure you know what qualitative and quantitative analyses are, and be ready to explain how you'd identify ionic compounds — remember you have to test for both the positive and the negative ion.

C3a Topic 1 — Qualitative Analysis

Testing for Ions

Q1 Robert adds a solution of **sodium hydroxide** to a solution of **calcium chloride**. The symbol for the calcium ion is Ca^{2+}.

a) What would Robert observe?

....

b) Write the balanced symbol equation for the reaction, including state symbols.

....

c) Write the balanced **ionic equation** for this reaction, including state symbols.

....

Q2 Cilla adds a few drops of **NaOH** solution to solutions of different **metal compounds**.

a) Complete her table of results.

Metal Cation	Colour of Precipitate
Fe^{2+}	
	blue
Fe^{3+}	
Al^{3+}	

b) Complete the balanced ionic equation for the reaction of iron(II) ions with hydroxide ions.

Fe^{2+}(............) + ... OH^-(aq) → .... (s)

c) Write a balanced **ionic** equation for the reaction of **iron(III) ions** with hydroxide ions.

....

Don't forget state symbols.

d) Cilla adds a few drops of sodium hydroxide solution to **aluminium sulfate solution**. She continues adding sodium hydroxide to excess. What would she observe at each stage?

....

....

Q3 Deirdre wants to find out if a soluble compound contains **chloride**, **bromide** or **iodide** ions. Explain how she could do this.

....

....

....

C3a Topic 1 — Qualitative Analysis

Testing for Ions

Q4 Select compounds from the box to match the following statements.

FeSO₄ contains the Fe²⁺ ion and FeCl₃ contains the Fe³⁺ ion.

| KCl | LiCl | FeSO$_4$ | NH$_4$Cl | FeCl$_3$ | Al$_2$(SO$_4$)$_3$ |
| NaCl | CuSO$_4$ | CaCl$_2$ | MgCl$_2$ | BaCl$_2$ | |

a) This compound forms a blue precipitate with sodium hydroxide solution. ....

b) This compound forms a white precipitate with sodium hydroxide that dissolves if excess sodium hydroxide is added. ....

c) This compound forms a green precipitate with sodium hydroxide solution. ....

d) This compound forms a brown precipitate with sodium hydroxide solution. ....

e) This compound reacts with sodium hydroxide to release a pungent gas. ....

f) This compound reacts with sodium hydroxide to form a white precipitate, and it also gives a brick-red flame in a flame test. ....

Q5 Claire was given a solid sample of a mixture of two ionic compounds. She was told that they were thought to be **ammonium chloride** and **calcium chloride**.

a) Describe, in detail, how she would test for the presence of the two **positive ions**.

....

....

....

b) What would she **observe** at each stage?

....

....

....

c) Write **ionic equations** for the reactions that identify the positive ions.

....

....

Top Tips: Right, this stuff needs to be learnt properly. Otherwise you'll be stuck in your exam staring at a question about the colour that some random solution goes when you add something you've never heard of before to it, and all you'll know is that ammonia smells of cat wee.

C3a Topic 1 — Qualitative Analysis

Measuring Amounts

Q1 a) Complete the following sentence.

> One mole of atoms or molecules of any substance will have a .... in grams equal to the .... for that substance.

b) Write down the **formula** for calculating the **mass** of a substance from the number of moles.

....

c) What is the **mass** of each of the following?

i) 1 mole of copper ....

ii) 3 moles of chlorine **gas** ....

iii) 2 moles of nitric acid (HNO_3) ....

iv) 2.5 moles of NaOH ....

v) 0.5 moles of calcium carbonate ($CaCO_3$) ....

Q2 a) Write down the formula for calculating the **number of moles in a given mass**.

....

b) How many **moles** are there in each of the following?

i) 20 g of calcium ....

ii) 112 g of sulfur ....

iii) 200 g of copper oxide (CuO) ....

iv) 110 g of carbon dioxide (CO_2) ....

c) Calculate the **mass** of each of the following.

i) 2 moles of sodium ....

ii) 1.25 moles of aluminium ....

iii) 0.75 moles of magnesium oxide (MgO) ....

iv) 0.025 moles of lead chloride ($PbCl_2$) ....

Top Tips: Everyone hates calculations but I'm afraid this page is full of them. Make sure you know which formula to use before you begin. Then do them all — it's the only way you'll get better.

C3a Topic 2 — Quantitative Analysis

Solutions and Concentrations

Q1 Complete the table by calculating the **mass-concentration** for each of these solutions.

MASS (g)	VOLUME	MASS–CONCENTRATION (g/dm^3)
2	4 dm^3	a)
4.6	2 dm^3	b)
0.8	500 cm^3	c)
0.2	100 cm^3	d)

Q2 Concentration can be measured in **moles/dm^3** or **g/dm^3**.

   a) Convert the following solution concentrations from moles/dm^3 to g/dm^3.

      i) 2 mol/dm^3 sodium hydroxide, NaOH.

      ....

      ....

      ii) 0.1 mol/dm^3 glucose, $C_6H_{12}O_6$.

      ....

      ....

   b) A solution of HCl has a mass-concentration of 3.8 g/dm^3. Calculate its mole-concentration.

   ....

   ....

Q3 Susan wants to work out the concentration of a solution of sodium chloride. She puts 10 g of the solution in a pre-weighed, clean, dry evaporating basin and heats the basin until all the water appears to have evaporated.

   a) What would Susan do next? Explain why she would do this.

   ....

   ....

   b) After doing this, how can she calculate the mass of sodium chloride that was dissolved?

   ....

   ....

C3a Topic 2 — Quantitative Analysis

Hard Water

Q1 Tick the correct boxes to show whether the statements are **true** or **false**.

		True	False
a)	Water can be softened by removing chloride and carbonate ions from the water.	☐	☐
b)	Adding sodium chloride is one way of removing hardness from water.	☐	☐
c)	When soap is used with hard water, it forms a lather easily.	☐	☐
d)	You can remove the hardness from water by adding sodium carbonate.	☐	☐

Q2 An **ion exchange resin** can be used to remove the hardness from water.

a) Circle the ions below that are responsible for causing hard water.

Ca^{2+} OH^- Ca^{3+} Mg^{2+} Na^+ Cl^- H^+

b) Explain how hard water becomes soft when it is passed through an **ion exchange resin**.

....

....

....

c) Does this method work for permanent hardness, temporary hardness, or both?

....

Q3 In an experiment to investigate the **causes** of **hardness** in water, soap solution was added to different solutions. Five drops were added at a time until a sustainable lather was formed.

Solution	Drops of soap solution needed to produce a lather	Observations
distilled water	5	no scum
magnesium sulfate solution	35	scum formed
calcium chloride solution	30	scum formed
sodium chloride solution	5	no scum

Distilled water has been purified to remove metal ions.

a) Why must all the solutions be prepared from distilled water rather than tap water?

....

....

b) i) Which compounds caused hardness in the water?

....

ii) Explain how you know.

....

C3a Topic 2 — Quantitative Analysis

Titrations

Q1 Circle the answer which best completes each of these sentences.

a) During acid-base titrations...

...methyl orange is always a suitable indicator.   ...the alkali must always go in the burette.

...the tap is opened fully near the end of the titration.   ...the flask is swirled regularly.

b) An acid-base titration is an example of a...

...precipitation reaction.   ...displacement reaction.

...neutralisation reaction.   ...reduction reaction.

c) Acid-base titrations are used to find...

...the rate of a reaction.   ...the concentration of an acid or base.

...the concentration of a salt.   ...the volume of a solution.

Q2 Circle the correct words below to complete the passage about how to do a titration.

Using a pipette and **measuring cylinder / pipette filler**, add some alkali to a conical flask, along with two or three drops of **indicator / litmus** solution. Using a **burette / pipette filler**, add acid to the alkali a bit at a time and give it a regular swirl. There's a colour change when all the alkali has been **dissolved / neutralised**. Record the **volume / temperature** of the **acid / alkali** used.

Q3 A **titration** procedure was used to compare the some fizzy drinks. The base used for the titration was sodium hydroxide solution.

a) Write down the **ionic equation** for this titration reaction.

....

fizzy drink	1st titre (cm^3)	2nd titre (cm^3)
Fizzade	15.2	14.6
Kolafizz	20.5	19.8
Cherriade	12.6	12.1

The titration values (titres) are shown in the table above.

b) Explain why the experiment was carried out twice.

....

c) Which drink contained the most acid?

....

C3a Topic 2 — Quantitative Analysis

More on Titrations

Q1 The concentration of some limewater, **Ca(OH)$_2$**, was determined by titration with hydrochloric acid, **HCl**. **50 cm^3** of limewater required **20 cm^3** of **0.1 mol/dm^3** hydrochloric acid to neutralise it. Work out the concentration of the limewater in **g/dm^3** using the steps outlined below.

a) How many moles of HCl are present in 20 cm^3 of 0.1 mol/dm^3 solution?

....

b) Complete the equation for the reaction.

.... + ... → CaCl$_2$ + ...

c) From the equation, ... mole(s) of HCl reacts with .... mole(s) of Ca(OH)$_2$.

d) Use your answers to **a)** and **c)** to work out how many moles of Ca(OH)$_2$ there are in 50 cm^3 of limewater.

....

e) What is the concentration of the limewater in **moles per dm^3**?

....

f) What is the concentration of the limewater in **grams per dm^3**?

....

Q2 In a titration, **10 cm^3** of sulfuric acid was used to neutralise **30 cm^3** of **0.1 mol/dm^3** potassium hydroxide solution.

$$H_2SO_4 + 2KOH \rightarrow K_2SO_4 + 2H_2O$$

a) Calculate the concentration of the sulfuric acid in **moles per dm^3**.

....

....

....

b) Calculate the concentration of the sulfuric acid in **grams per dm^3**.

....

....

Top Tips: Aargh, not more calculations... As if Chemistry wasn't tricky enough without some maths getting involved too (but at least it's not as bad as Physics). Actually, these aren't the worst calculations — as long as you remember to tackle them in stages and you know your equations.

C3a Topic 2 — Quantitative Analysis

Preparing Soluble Salts

Q1 Nickel sulfate (a soluble salt) was made by adding **insoluble nickel carbonate** to **sulfuric acid** until no further reaction occurred.

a) State how you would know when the reaction is complete.

....

Once the reaction was complete, the excess nickel carbonate was separated from the nickel sulfate solution using the apparatus shown.

b) Label the diagram which shows the separation process.

....

....

....

c) What is this method of separation called?

....

d) Describe how you could produce a solid sample of nickel sulfate from nickel sulfate solution.

....

....

e) Potassium hydroxide is a **soluble salt**. It reacts with sulfuric acid to form **potassium sulfate**.

i) Explain **why** the method used to make nickel sulfate needs to be modified for this reaction.

....

....

....

ii) Explain **how** you would modify the method.

....

....

....

C3a Topic 2 — Quantitative Analysis

C3a Topic 3 — Electrolytic Processes

Electrolysis of Molten Substances

Q1 Explain why the **electrolyte** needs to be either a **solution** or **molten** for electrolysis to work.

....

....

....

Q2 **Molten sodium chloride** can be split up by electrolysis.

a) Tick the boxes to show whether the following statements are **true** or **false**.   True   False

   i) The chloride ions are oxidised. ☐ ☐

   ii) Chloride ions are attracted to the negative cathode. ☐ ☐

   iii) The sodium ions are reduced. ☐ ☐

   iv) Sodium ions are attracted to the positive anode. ☐ ☐

   v) Electrolysis always involves either reduction or oxidation, never both. ☐ ☐

b) State two uses for the sodium made by electrolysis.

   1. ....

   2. ....

Q3 **Molten lead bromide** ($PbBr_2$) is electrolysed using inert electrodes.

a) i) Give the **anion** in this reaction. ....

   ii) Write the half-equation for the reaction at the **anode**. ....

b) i) Give the **cation** in this reaction. ....

   ii) Write the half-equation for the reaction at the **cathode**. ....

Q4 **Complete** and **balance** the following electrode reactions.
For each one, tick the correct box to show whether it is **oxidation** or **reduction**.

                                                                         Oxidation   Reduction

a) Na^+ + ... → ....   ☐   ☐

b) Cu^{2+} + ...e^- → ....   ☐   ☐

c) ....OH^- → ....H_2O + O_2 + ...e^- ☐   ☐

Electrolysis of Solutions

Q1 The diagram below shows the electrolysis of a **salt solution**.

a) Identify the ions and molecules labelled A, B, C and D on the diagram. Choose from the options in the box below.

| Na⁺ | H⁺ | Cl₂ | H₂ |
| Cl⁻ | Na₂ | H₂O | OH⁻ |

A .... B ....

C .... D ....

b) Write **balanced** half-equations for the processes that occur during the electrolysis of this salt solution.

Cathode: ....

Anode: ....

Make sure the charges balance.

Q2 Electrolysis using **inert electrodes** was carried out on a number of different compounds.

Complete the table to predict the products formed during electrolysis of the compounds. Include the state symbols.

Compound	Product formed at the:	
	cathode	anode
copper chloride solution		
copper sulfate solution		
sodium sulfate solution		

Q3 Explain why the electrolysis of **molten** ionic salts is different from salts in **solution**.

....

....

....

....

C3a Topic 3 — Electrolytic Processes

Electrolysis Using Copper Electrodes

Q1 Why would it **not** be a good idea to carry out the electrolysis of **copper** in an electrolyte that contained **zinc** ions instead of copper ions? Tick the correct box.

The zinc ions will not conduct an electrical current. ☐

The copper produced will have zinc impurities in it. ☐

A poisonous gas would be produced. ☐

The zinc and copper ions will react with each other. ☐

The zinc ions will coat the anode. ☐

Q2 The diagram below shows the purification of **copper** by electrolysis.

a) Identify the labels A to D on the diagram. Choose from the options in the box.

| copper ions | copper atoms | impure copper electrode |
| copper sulfate solution | pure copper electrode | batteries |

A ....

B ....

C ....

D ....

b) Write down the half equations for the reactions at:

i) the anode ....

ii) the cathode ....

c) When copper is purified by electrolysis, **impure sludge** simply falls to the bottom. It does **not** move to the cathode. Suggest why this happens.

Think about why substances move between the electrodes.

....

....

d) The table below shows the mass of the two electrodes before and after the experiment.

	Electrode A (mass in g)	Electrode B (mass in g)
Before	122.6	19.7
After	34.0	113.9

Which electrode is the anode? Explain your answer.

....

....

C3a Topic 3 — Electrolytic Processes

Electroplating

Q1 Fill in the gaps in the passage below using some of the words from the box.

| gold | appearance | carbon | unreactive | strong | malleability | corroding |

There are a number of reasons why metals are electroplated. Jewellery can be electroplated with .... to improve the .... of the metal. Other metals can be electroplated to stop them .... Metals used for this reason must be ....

Q2 Lily is carrying out an experiment to electroplate **zinc** onto a **copper rod**.

a) Which material should Lily use for:

i) the anode? ....

ii) the cathode? ....

b) i) Circle the compound in the list below that Lily should use as the electrolyte.

    copper sulfate   **hydrochloric acid**   **zinc sulfate**

ii) Explain your choice.

....

....

Q3 Electroplating could be used to put a thin coat of **silver** onto a **nickel** fork.

a) Complete the diagram by labelling the **cathode** and **anode**.

b) What ion must the electrolyte contain?

....

c) Give the half equation for the reaction at:

i) the anode ....

ii) the cathode ....

Top Tips: Electroplating is an important use for electrolysis in the real world. The trick with an electroplating question is to make sure you're clear about which metal is being to plated onto which. The electrolyte will have to contain the ions of the plating metal or the whole thing won't work.

C3a Topic 3 — Electrolytic Processes

Mixed Questions — C3a Topics 1, 2 & 3

Q1 'Test The Water' are a company who measure the purity of tap water. They analysed a 238 cm³ sample of water and find that it contains **0.1 g of iron**.

a) What is the **mass-concentration** of iron in the water?

....

....

b) Was the analysis carried out **qualitative** or **quantitative**?

....

Q2 Sam is taking part in a chemistry competition where she needs to be able to identify various **ions**.

a) Sam has a flowchart to help her identify **halide ions** present in a water sample. Complete the gaps in her flowchart.

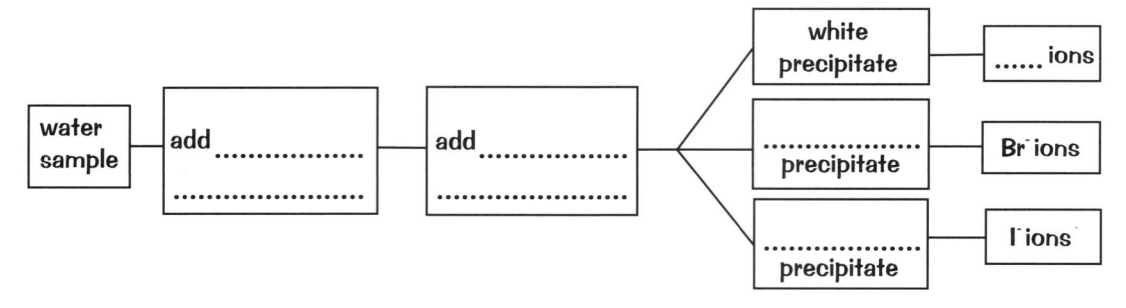

[Flowchart: water sample → add .... → add .... → white precipitate → ...... ions / .... precipitate → Br⁻ ions / .... precipitate → I⁻ ions]

b) What type of analysis would this be? ....

c) Sam has another flowchart for identifying **positive ions**. Fill in the gaps.

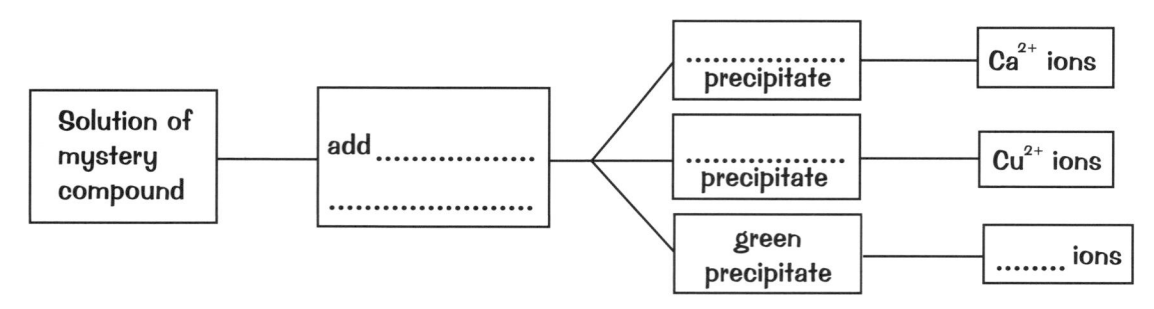

[Flowchart: Solution of mystery compound → add .... → .... precipitate → Ca²⁺ ions / .... precipitate → Cu²⁺ ions / green precipitate → .... ions]

d) Sam knows that if she adds sodium hydroxide solution to a solution of aluminium ions, there will be a white precipitate which will then redissolve in excess sodium hydroxide to form a colourless solution. Write the ionic equations including state symbols for these two reactions.

....

....

C3a Topic 3 — Electrolytic Processes

Mixed Questions — C3a Topics 1, 2 & 3

Q3 Magnesium reacts with nitric acid, HNO$_3$, to form **magnesium nitrate**, Mg(NO$_3$)$_2$, and hydrogen.

a) Work out the relative formula mass of magnesium nitrate.

....

b) When 0.12 g of magnesium reacted with excess acid, 0.74 g of magnesium nitrate was formed.

  i) Calculate the number of moles of magnesium that reacted and the number of moles of magnesium nitrate produced.

  ....

  ....

  ii) If 0.025 moles of nitric acid was used, what mass of nitric acid was this?

  ....

Q4 Hyde tested samples of water from three different **rivers** using the following method.

> 8 cm^3 of river water was placed in a test tube.
> 1 cm^3 of soap solution was added and the tube was shaken.
> More soap was added until a <u>lasting lather</u> was produced.
> The amount of soap solution needed was recorded.
> The experiment was repeated with boiled water from the river.

The results of the experiment are shown in the table.

RIVER	AMOUNT OF SOAP NEEDED (cm^3)	
	PLAIN WATER	BOILED WATER
A	7	5
B	2	2
C	4	4

a) Which river contained the softest water? ....

b) Which river contained the hardest water? ....

c) Why was less soap needed to form a lasting lather after the water from river A was boiled?

....

....

....

d) The hardness in rivers B and C could not be removed by boiling.

  i) State the name given to this type of hardness.

  ....

  ii) Suggest one way of removing the hardness from rivers B and C.

  ....

C3a Topic 3 — Electrolytic Processes

Calculating Volumes

Q1 a) What is the **volume** of **one mole** of any gas at room temperature and pressure? Circle your answer.

      24 dm³   12 dm³   2.4 dm³   36 dm³

b) What is the name given to this volume? Circle your answer.

    mass volume   room volume   Avogadro's volume   molar volume

c) What volume is occupied by the following gases at room temperature and pressure?

  i) 0.5 moles of hydrogen chloride. ....

  ii) 6.25 moles of ammonia. ....

d) How many moles are there in the following gases at room temperature and pressure?

  i) 240 cm³ of hydrogen. ....

  ii) 8 dm³ of chlorine. ....

Q2 The **limewater test** for carbon dioxide involves the reaction between carbon dioxide and calcium hydroxide, which is shown in the following equation:

$$CO_{2\,(g)} + Ca(OH)_{2\,(aq)} \rightarrow CaCO_{3\,(s)} + H_2O_{(l)}$$

RTP stands for 'room temperature and pressure'.

A solution of limewater containing 0.37 g of calcium hydroxide reacts with carbon dioxide at RTP.

a) What mass of **carbon dioxide** is needed to react completely with the limewater?

....

....

b) What **volume** does this amount of carbon dioxide occupy at RTP?

....

Q3 **Sulfur dioxide** (SO_2) is a gas produced when sulfur burns in oxygen.

a) Write down the **chemical equation** for this reaction.

....

b) Calculate the relative molecular mass (M_r) of SO_2.

....

c) Calculate the **volume** of sulfur dioxide produced when **144 g** of sulfur burns in oxygen.

....

....

....

Reversible Reactions

Q1 Use words from the list below to complete the following sentences about **reversible reactions**.

| escape | reactants | closed | products | react | balance |

a) In a reversible reaction, the .... of the reaction can themselves .... to give the original ....

b) At equilibrium, the amounts of reactants and products reach a ....

c) To reach equilibrium the reaction must happen in a .... system where products and reactants can't ....

Q2 Which of these statements about reversible reactions are **true** and which are **false**? True False

a) The position of an equilibrium depends on the reaction conditions. ☐ ☐

b) Upon reaching a dynamic equilibrium, the reactions stop taking place. ☐ ☐

c) You can move the position of equilibrium to get more product. ☐ ☐

d) At equilibrium there will always be equal quantities of products and reactants. ☐ ☐

Q3 Look at this diagram of a **reversible reaction**.

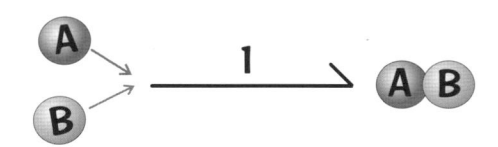

a) For the forward reaction:
   i) give the reactant(s) ....
   ii) give the product(s) ....

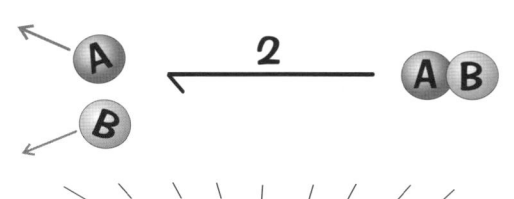

b) Here are two labels:

   X product splits up
   Y reactants combine

   The reaction going from left to right is called the forward reaction.
   The reaction going from right to left is called the backward reaction.

   i) Which of these labels goes in position 1 — X or Y? ....
   ii) Which goes in position 2 — X or Y? ....

c) Write the equation for the reversible reaction. ....

d) Complete the sentence by circling the correct phrase:

   In a dynamic equilibrium, the forward and backward reactions are happening: **at different rates** / **at zero rate** / **at the same rate**.

C3b Topic 4 — Gases, Reversible Reactions and Ammonia

Reversible Reactions

Q4 Substances A and B react to produce substances C and D in a **reversible reaction**.

$$2A(g) + B(g) \rightleftharpoons 2C(g) + D(g)$$

a) The forward reaction is **exothermic**. Does the backward reaction give out or take in heat? Explain your answer.

....

....

b) If the temperature is raised, will the equilibrium position move to the left or to the right?

....

c) Explain why changing the **temperature** of a reversible reaction always affects the position of the equilibrium.

....

....

d) Explain the effect of changing the **pressure** on the position of equilibrium in this reaction.

....

....

Q5 Look at the equation showing another **reversible reaction**.

$$2SO_2(g) + O_2(g) \rightleftharpoons 2SO_3(g)$$

a) i) Explain which reaction, forward or backward, is accompanied by a **decrease** in volume.

....

....

ii) How will increasing the pressure affect the position of equilibrium in this reaction?

....

....

b) What does adding a catalyst to a reversible reaction do? Circle the letter next to your answer.

    A   It moves the equilibrium position towards the products.

    B   It makes the reaction reach equilibrium more quickly.

    C   It moves the equilibrium position towards the reactants.

    D   It causes a decrease in pressure.

c) What happens to the amount of product at equilibrium when you use a catalyst?

....

C3b Topic 4 — Gases, Reversible Reactions and Ammonia

The Haber Process

Q1 The Haber process is used to make **ammonia**. The equation for the reaction is:

$$N_2(g) + 3H_2(g) \rightleftharpoons 2NH_3(g)$$

a) Name the reactants in the forward reaction. ....

b) Which side of the equation has more molecules? ....

c) How should the pressure be changed in order to produce more ammonia? Explain your answer.

....

....

Q2 The **industrial conditions** for the Haber process are shown below.

Pressure: 200 atmospheres   Temperature: 450 °C

a) Suggest why a pressure greater than 200 atmospheres is not used.

....

b) In the Haber process reaction, the **forward** reaction is **exothermic**.

   i) What effect will raising the temperature have on the **amount** of ammonia formed?

   ....

   ii) Explain why a high temperature is used industrially.

   ....

   ....

Q3 Stuart is a farmer. He uses **fertilisers** manufactured from ammonia to help his plants grow.

a) What name is given to fertilisers manufactured from ammonia?

....

b) Some of the fertiliser used by Stuart is washed into a lake next to his land.
Explain the possible **environmental consequences** of this.

....

....

....

....

C3b Topic 4 — Gases, Reversible Reactions and Ammonia

C3b Topic 5 — Organic Chemistry

Homologous Series

Q1 Fill in the gaps in the passage below using the words from the box.

| physical | elements | chemical | general | boiling points | molecular |

A homologous series is a group of compounds with the same .... formula. This means that the compounds contain the same .... and have similar .... structures. The compounds have similar .... properties but show gradual variation in their .... properties. For example, the .... of compounds in a homologous series increase as their size increases.

Q2 Below are the names of four different **hydrocarbons** from the same homologous series.

a) Write the molecular formula and draw the structural formula for the following hydrocarbons. One has been done for you.

Name	Molecular formula	Structural formula
methane	....	
ethane	C_2H_6	H-C-C-H with H's above and below each C
propane	....	
butane	....	

b) What name is given to this family of hydrocarbons?

....

Homologous Series

Q3 The **structural formulas** of alcohols can be used to identify them and determine their **properties**.

a) Circle any of the following molecular and structural formulas that represent alcohols.

C_4H_{10}

H-C(H,H)-C(=O)(OH)

H-C(H,H)-C(H,H)-C(H,H)-O-H

C_3H_7COOH

H-C(H,H)-C(H,H)-C(H,H)-H

C_2H_5OH

b) State the **general formula** for alcohols.

....

Q4 All **carboxylic acids** react in a similar way.

a) In the space below draw the **structural formula** of methanoic acid.

b) Write down the **molecular formula** for:

i) propanoic acid. ....

ii) ethanoic acid. ....

Q5 Alkenes contain **carbon** and **hydrogen** atoms only.

a) State the **general formula** of alkenes.

....

b) Draw lines to match the name of the alkene to its structural formula.

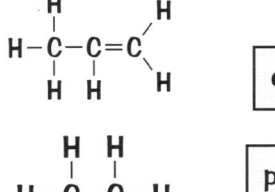

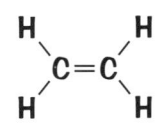

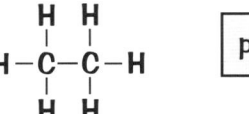

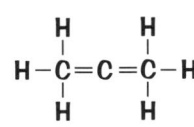

H-C(H,H)-C(H)=C(H,H) | ethene | C(H,H)=C(H,H)

H-C(H,H)-C(H,H)-H | propene | H-C(H,H)=C=C(H,H)-H

c) Describe how the structure of an alkene is different from the structure of an alkane.

....

C3b Topic 5 — Organic Chemistry

Production of Ethanol

Q1 Ethanol is produced using **fermentation**.

a) Complete the following sentences by choosing the correct words from the list below.

| concentration | carbohydrates | ethene | anaerobic |
| enzyme | aerobic | temperature | ester |

i) Fermentation is used to turn .... into ethanol.

ii) The reaction happens due to an .... found in yeast.

iii) The .... needs to be carefully controlled during the reaction.

iv) The process of fermentation is carried out under .... conditions.

b) Which of the following is the correct equation for the production of ethanol from glucose? Circle A, B, C or D.

A $C_6H_{12}O_6 \rightarrow 2C_2H_5OH + 2CO_2$

B $C_6H_{12}O_6 \rightarrow 2C_2H_5OH + 2O_2$

C $C_6H_{12}O_6 \rightarrow 2C_2H_5OH + H_2O$

D $C_6H_{12}O_6 \rightarrow 2C_2H_5OH + 2CH_4$

Q2 Describe how you would produce a solution of ethanol by **fermentation** in the laboratory.

....

....

....

....

....

....

C3b Topic 5 — Organic Chemistry

Production of Ethanol

Q3 The diagram below shows the **apparatus** that can be used to further process the ethanol solution produced by fermentation.

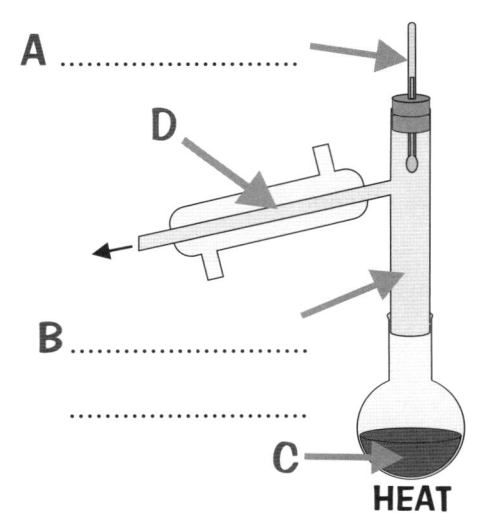

a) What is the name of this process?

....

b) i) Label the pieces of equipment marked A and B.

ii) Describe what happens at the following places on the diagram.

C ....

D ....

c) Explain why this further processing is necessary.

....

....

Q4 Fermentation uses yeast to produce ethanol.

a) Outline one **advantage** of using fermentation to produce ethanol.

....

....

b) Give one **disadvantage** of making ethanol by fermentation.

....

....

C3b Topic 5 — Organic Chemistry

Production and Issues of Ethanol

Q1 Fermentation is not used for **large-scale production** of high quality **ethanol**.

    a) Which of the following is the correct word equation for the reaction used to produce ethanol? Circle the correct answer.

        ethane + steam → ethanol   ethanoic acid + steam → ethanol

        ethyl ethanoate + steam → ethanol   ethene + steam → ethanol

    b) Give one **advantage** of using this method to produce ethanol.

        ....

Q2 Rachel is giving a presentation in class about the impacts of excessive alcohol drinking on society.

Rachel says: "Getting drunk can lead to vandalism and violence."

Suggest three other costs to **society** of excessive alcohol drinking.

    1. ....

    2. ....

    3. ....

Q3 Excessive **alcohol** intake can have **damaging effects** on the human body.

Describe the damaging effects that alcohol may have on the body.

....

....

....

....

....

....

C3b Topic 5 — Organic Chemistry

Ethene and Ethanoic Acid

Q1 Ethanol can be used to make **ethene**.

a) Write a symbol equation for the conversion of ethanol into ethene.

....

b) Circle the correct word below to show the name of this process.

      dehydration   polymerisation   oxidation   cracking

Q2 Wine that has been left open to the air for several days often tastes like **vinegar**.

a) Explain why wine that has been left open tastes like vinegar.

....

....

b) State one use for vinegar.

....

Q3 **Ethanoic acid** displays the reactions of a typical acid.

a) i) Write the word equation for the reaction between ethanoic acid and calcium.

....

ii) Write the symbol equation for this reaction.

....

b) Fill in the gaps to complete the symbol equation below for the reaction between ethanoic acid and the base potassium hydroxide.

    .... + KOH ⟶ .... + ...

c) Circle the products below that are formed in the reaction between ethanoic acid and sodium carbonate.

    | hydrogen | | sodium ethanoate | | water |

    | sodium chloride | | carbon dioxide | | oxygen |

d) Describe the effect of ethanoic acid on litmus paper.

....

C3b Topic 5 — Organic Chemistry

Esters

Q1 Recycled **polyesters** are used in the manufacture of clothing.

a) Circle the clothing material below that can be made using recycled polyester.

wool   cotton   fleece   denim

b) Name one other use for polyesters, apart from in clothing.

....

Q2 Hermione works for a **perfume manufacturer**. She frequently uses **esters**, since they are commonly used in perfume production.

a) Give one property of esters that make them suited for use in perfumes.

....

b) Part of Hermione's job involves producing an ester called ethyl ethanoate.

Which of the following represents the correct reaction for the production of ethyl ethanoate? Circle the correct answer.

ethanol + water → ethyl ethanoate + carbon dioxide

ethanol + ethane → ethyl ethanoate + water

magnesium oxide + ethanoic acid → ethyl ethanoate + water

ethanol + ethanoic acid → ethyl ethanoate + water

c) In the space below, draw the structural formula of **ethyl ethanoate**.

d) Other than perfumes, give one use of esters in the chemical industry.

....

Esther — also runs for parliament

Top Tips: Esters really are great, but they don't only occur in industry. The smells and flavours of most fruits are caused by esters. Make sure you've got the basics under your hat, like the general word equation for the formation of an ester and all the different uses of esters.

C3b Topic 5 — Organic Chemistry

Uses of Esters

Q1 Soaps and detergents are made from **fatty acids**.

a) Fill in the gaps to complete the sentences below.

   i) Fats and oils are types of ....

   ii) Soaps are made by .... oils and fats

   in a concentrated .... solution.

b) The diagram below shows a labelled **soap anion**.

hydrophilic head → ●〰〰〰 ← hydrophobic tail

Which section of the molecule is attracted to:

i) water molecules? ....

ii) grease and oil? ....

c) Describe how soap molecules lift oily stains out of fabric.

....

....

....

Q2 Unsaturated oils can be converted into solid saturated fats.

a) Explain what is meant by the terms **saturated oil** and **unsaturated oil**.

....

....

b) i) What is the name of the process used to convert liquid oils into saturated fats?

....

ii) Describe what happens to the unsaturated oils during this process.

....

....

....

c) Name one product in the food industry that is made using this process.

....

C3b Topic 5 — Organic Chemistry

Mixed Questions — C3b Topics 4 & 5

Q1 Ethanol can be produced by fermentation or by the hydration of ethene.

a) Write the word equation for the fermentation of glucose.

....

b) Describe an advantage that the hydration of ethene has over fermentation.

....

c) At the moment, the production of ethanol by hydration of ethene is a cheap process. Explain why it will soon become more expensive.

....

....

....

Q2 Avogadro's Law is used to calculate the volume of a gas.

a) State Avogadro's law.

....

....

b) The chemical equation for the formation of hydrogen peroxide is shown below.

$$H_{2(g)} + O_{2(g)} \rightarrow H_2O_{2(g)}$$

Volume of gas (dm³) = $\frac{\text{Mass of gas (g)}}{M_r \text{ of gas}} \times 24$

i) Find the volume of hydrogen peroxide produced when 3.8 g of oxygen reacts with hydrogen.

....

....

....

....

ii) What volume of hydrogen is needed to produce this volume of hydrogen peroxide?

....

c) Calculate the volume of 6.2 moles of H_2O_2 at room temperature and pressure.

....

....

C3b Topic 5 — Organic Chemistry

Mixed Questions — C3b Topics 4 & 5

Q3 If exposed to the air, **ethanol** in wine is converted to **ethanoic acid**.

a) i) State the word equation for the formation of ethanoic acid from ethanol.

....

ii) What type of reaction is this? Circle the word from the list below.

| oxidation | neutralisation | reduction | dehydration |

The chemical formula for sodium carbonate is Na_2CO_3.

b) Write down the balanced symbol equation for the reaction between ethanoic acid and sodium carbonate.

....

Q4 The Paper Street Soap Company make soaps by reacting **esters** with **sodium hydroxide**.

a) i) Esters are an example of a **homologous series**.
Describe what is meant by the term 'homologous series'.

....

....

ii) Describe how the boiling points of esters change as the size of the molecules **increases**.

....

b) i) State the word equation for the formation of an ester from the reaction between ethanoic acid and ethanol.

....

ii) Draw the structural formula equation for the reaction between ethanoic acid and ethanol.

c) Describe how an ester and sodium hydroxide are used to produce soap.

....

....

....

C3b Topic 5 — Organic Chemistry

Medical Physics and Ultrasound

Q1 In each of the following sentences, circle the correct word(s) from each highlighted pair.

a) X-rays are **low / high** energy electromagnetic waves.

b) X-rays are **transmitted / absorbed** by soft tissue but are **transmitted / absorbed** by dense material such as bone.

c) X-rays are a type of **ionising / non-ionising** radiation.

Q2 Tick the boxes to show whether each of these statements is **true** or **false**.

	True	False
a) CAT scans can produce an image of a 2D 'slice' of the body.	☐	☐
b) Only soft tissue can be imaged by CAT scans.	☐	☐
c) CAT scans use ultrasound waves.	☐	☐
d) Ionising radiation is used to produce a CAT scan.	☐	☐
e) CAT scans are typically used to check fetal development.	☐	☐

Q3 A concentrated beam of **ultrasound** can be used to treat kidney stones.

a) What is ultrasound?

....

....

b) What effect does the ultrasound beam have on kidney stones?

....

c) How are the kidney stone remains removed from the body?

....

d) Give two reasons why using ultrasound is a good way of treating kidney stones.

1. ....

2. ....

e) Describe **one** other medical use of ultrasound.

....

....

P3a Topic 1 — Radiation and Treatment

Intensity of Radiation

Q1 The word '**radiation**' is often used to refer to nuclear sources, but it also covers many other types.

    a) Sort the following forms of radiation according to their properties.

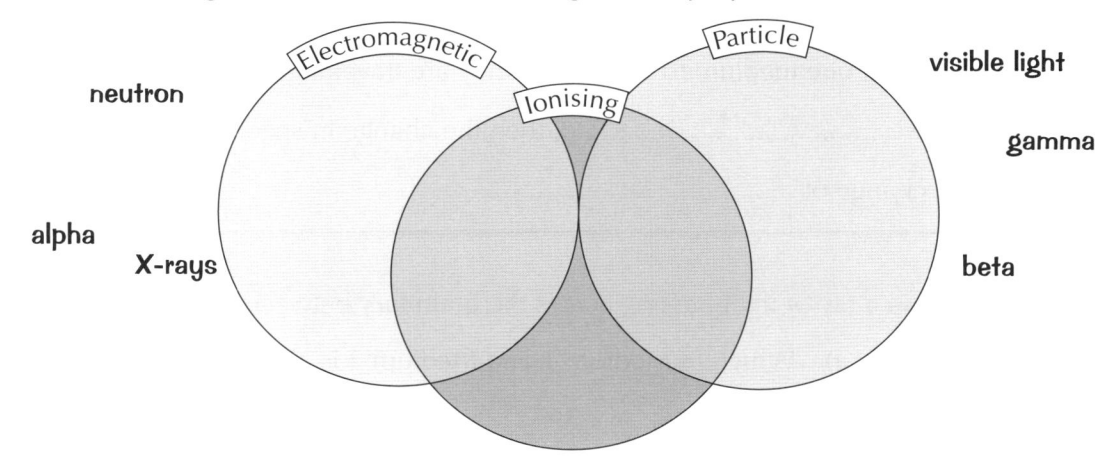

(Venn diagram with three overlapping circles labelled Electromagnetic, Ionising, Particle. Items to sort: neutron, alpha, X-rays, visible light, gamma, beta)

    b) What is the definition of radiation?

....

Q2 Tick the boxes to show whether each of these statements is **true** or **false**.   True   False

    a) The intensity of radiation depends on the medium it has passed through. ☐ ☐

    b) A vacuum absorbs some of the radiation passing through it. ☐ ☐

    c) Generally, the less dense the medium, the more radiation that is absorbed. ☐ ☐

Q3 Sam and Amy have made a spherical lantern for the Halloween parade. The lantern has a **diameter** of **40 cm** and contains a candle with a power of **0.8 W** at its centre.

    a) Calculate the surface area of the lantern, in square metres.

Remember the surface area of a sphere = $4/3 \pi r^2$

....

....

    b) Calculate the **intensity** of the light radiation on the inside surface of the lantern.

....

    c) How will the intensity of the light from the candle reaching the outside surface of the lantern compare to that reaching the inside surface? Explain your answer.

....

....

Top Tips: If this intensity of radiation malarkey is just not making sense, try getting a torch out and seeing it in action. Hold your hand up close to the torch, what do you see — a bright spot of light. Shine it on the fence at the bottom of the garden, guess what — a large patch of dim light.

P3a Topic 1 — Radiation and Treatment

Lenses

Q1 Fill in the blanks in the passage below.

> Waves can speed up or .... when they
> pass from one medium to another. If they are travelling at an angle
> to the .... then the change in speed results
> in a change of ....

Q2 The diagram shows a ray of light passing across the **boundary** between two media.

a) Which of Medium 1 and Medium 2 is air and which is glass?

Medium 1 is .... **Medium 2 is** ....

b) Explain your answer to **a**). ....

....

Q3 In the ray diagrams below, the pictures of the lenses have been removed.

a) What type of lens could this be? Underline the correct answer from the options below.

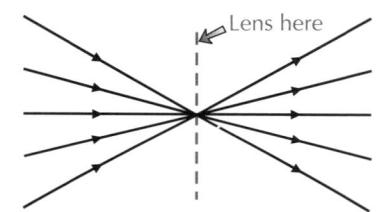

- **A** A converging lens
- **B** A diverging lens
- **C** Neither a converging nor a diverging lens
- **D** Either a converging or a diverging lens

b) On the diagram to the right, draw a lens of the correct type in the right position to complete the ray diagram.

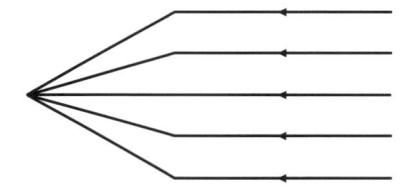

Q4 The diagram shows a **diverging lens**.

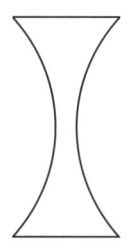

a) Draw the path of a ray passing through the lens **along the axis** from left to right.

b) Draw the paths of two incident rays **parallel** to the first ray, one **above** and one **below** the axis.

c) Sketch in the position of the **virtual focal point** for the rays shown and label it "F".

P3a Topic 1 — Radiation and Treatment

Lenses

Q5 This question is about how to **draw ray diagrams** to show an image formed by a **converging** lens.

a) The first step is to draw a ray from the **top** of the object going **parallel** to the **axis** of the lens. Where does this ray pass through when it's refracted?

....

b) The next step is to draw a ray from the top of the object which passes through the lens **without** being refracted. Where does this ray pass through the lens?

....

c) How do the steps above tell you where the **top** of the **image** will be on the ray diagram?

....

Q6 Draw a ray diagram to locate where the image is by **following the instructions** below.

a) Draw a ray from the **top** of the object (towards the lens) **parallel** to the axis, and continue the path of the ray through the lens.

b) Draw a ray from the top of the object passing through the **centre** of the lens.

c) Mark the **top** of the image.

d) Mark the **bottom** of the image, and draw in the image.

e) Now **describe** the image fully.

Take these ray diagrams step by step. Make sure you draw them really carefully, with a ruler.

....

....

....

Top Tips:
There are a lot of technical terms when it comes to lenses and ray diagrams — 'inverted', 'virtual image' and 'focal point' to name just a few. Take your time over these pages and make sure you're completely comfortable with not only drawing ray diagrams, but interpreting them too.

P3a Topic 1 — Radiation and Treatment

Lenses

Q7 Complete this ray diagram so that you can **fully describe** the image that this lens produces.

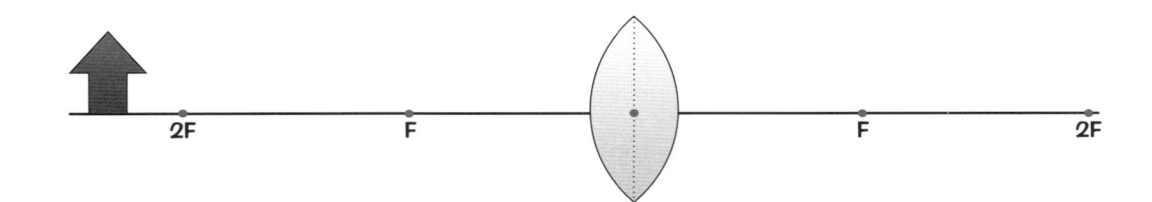

Description of image: ....
....
....

Q8 An aubergine is placed 6.1 cm away from a converging lens with a focal length of **7 cm**.

a) Will the image formed by the lens be:

i) upright or inverted? ....

ii) on the same side of the lens or on the opposite side? ....

iii) real or virtual? ....

b) The aubergine is now placed at a distance X from the lens. The image is now bigger than the object and inverted. Which of the options below could be distance X? Circle your answer.

A 3.9 cm   B 7.0 cm   C 10.2 cm   D 14.0 cm   E 15.3 cm

Q9 Circle the correct options in this description of images formed by **diverging lenses**.

Diverging lenses always produce **real / virtual**, **upright / inverted**

images which are **smaller / larger** than the object.

Q10 The diagram below shows an object placed next to a diverging lens. The focal points are marked.

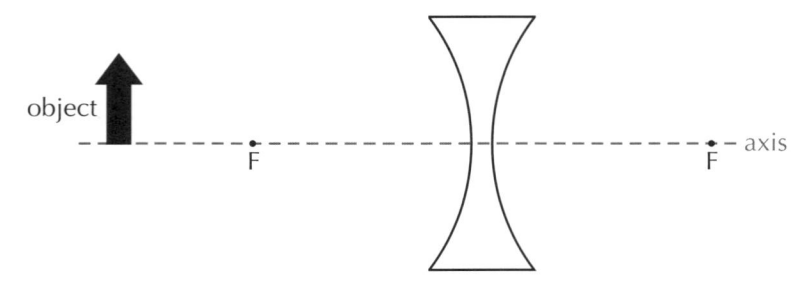

a) On the diagram, draw the path of a ray coming from the top of the object and travelling in the direction of the centre of the lens.

b) Draw the path of a ray coming from the top of the object and going towards the focal point on the far side of the lens.

c) Draw the image formed by the lens.

P3a Topic 1 — Radiation and Treatment

Power and the Lens Equation

Q1 Dave is using a converging lens to **focus** some parallel rays of light to a point.

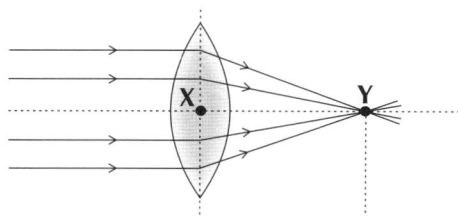

a) If the distance between the centre of the lens, X, and the focal point, Y, is 15 cm, what is the power of the lens?

....

b) Dave wants to increase the distance between the lens and the focal point, so he switches the lens for one with a power of +5.2 D. Calculate the new distance between X and Y.

....

....

c) Assuming they are made of the same material, how will the lens Dave uses in part **b)** look different to the one in part **a)**?

....

....

Q2 The **lens equation** can be used to find the position of an image created by a **converging lens**.

a) **i)** Write the lens equation that links the letters f, v and u.

....

ii) Write down what the letters f, v and u stand for in the equation you wrote in **a) i)**.

f = ... v = ... u = ...

b) An armadillo squats **0.5 m** from a converging lens of focal length **0.6 m**.

i) Use the lens equation to calculate the **distance** of the **image** of the armadillo from the lens.

....

....

....

ii) **Describe** the image of the armadillo.

....

....

P3a Topic 1 — Radiation and Treatment

The Eye

Q1 Write **labels** in the spaces to complete the diagram of a human eye.

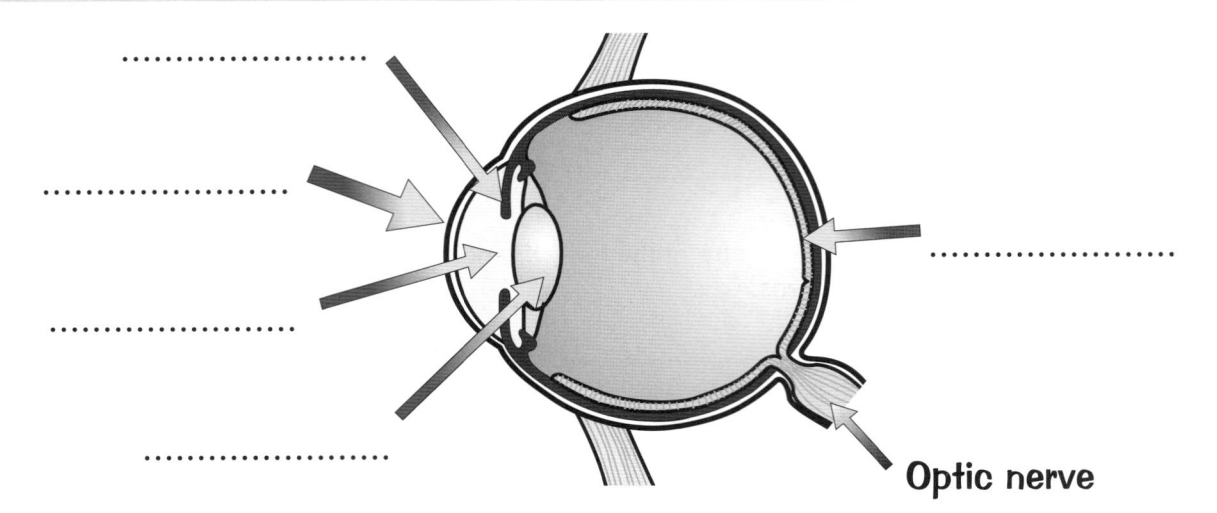

.... Optic nerve

Q2 **Complete the table** about the functions of different parts of the eye.

Part of the eye	Function
....	Focuses light on the retina
Retina	....
Ciliary muscles	....
....	Hole through which light enters the eye

Q3 Circle the correct word in each pair to complete the passage below.

When you look at distant objects, your ciliary muscles **contract / relax**, and pull the lens to make it **thin / fat**. The opposite actions happen when you look at near objects. The combined action of the lens and **cornea / iris** focuses the light on the **pupil / retina** to produce an image. Cells on the **pupil / retina** send signals to the brain to be interpreted via the optic nerve.

P3a Topic 1 — Radiation and Treatment

The Eye

Q4 The range of human eyesight lies between the **near** and **far points**.
Complete the definitions of near and far points and give an **estimated value** for each.

a) i) The near point is ....

ii) For normally-sighted adults, the near point is about .... cm.

b) i) The far point is ....

ii) For normally-sighted adults, the far point is at ....

Q5 Common vision problems are caused by the eye focusing an image in the wrong place.

a) Look at the diagram on the right. Complete the sentences by circling the correct word(s) from the highlighted options.

This person, with this vision defect, is **short / long** sighted.

The **near / far** point is closer than infinity, which makes

it difficult to focus on things that are **close up / far away**.

The object in the diagram is brought into focus **in front of / behind** the retina.

b) Give **two possible causes** of the problem shown in the diagram.

1. ....

2. ....

Q6 James has just been diagnosed as **long-sighted**.

a) i) Describe how being long-sighted affects James' near point.

....

ii) A correctly focused eye will form an image of near and far objects exactly on the retina. Where will James' eyes form a focused image of a nearby object?

....

b) Give two possible **causes** of James' long sight.

1. ....

2. ....

P3a Topic 1 — Radiation and Treatment

Correcting Vision Defects

Q1 Short sight can be corrected by placing a lens in front of the cornea.

a) Which of the two lenses shown below could correct this problem? Circle the correct letter.

A   B

b) Explain how the lens you chose in part **a)** would help to correct the eye problem.

....

....

....

Q2 Lasers are used in corrective **eye surgery**.

a) Describe how can a laser be used to correct long sight.

....

....

b) Laser eye surgery is becoming an increasingly popular way to correct vision problems.

i) Give one advantage of having laser eye surgery to correct vision instead of using glasses.

....

ii) Describe two disadvantages of using laser correction instead of glasses to correct vision.

1. ....

....

2. ....

....

c) Name **one other way** in which long sight could be corrected.
Explain how this method of correction works.

....

....

Top Tips: Long sight is something that a lot of people suffer from as they get older. Once you get beyond the age of around 40, the lenses in your eyes get stiffer and lose their ability to change shape to become fat enough to focus on things close up. That's why a lot of older people need glasses to read — their lenses don't have the flexibility to focus on the words.

P3a Topic 1 — Radiation and Treatment

Snell's Law and Total Internal Reflection

Q1 Here is a diagram of a ray of light entering a material with **refractive index, n**.

a) Label the following parts of the diagram:

Incident ray   Normal   Refracted ray

Angle of incidence, i   Angle of refraction, r

b) Snell's law relates the refractive index, **n** to the two angles **i** and **r**. Write down Snell's law.

....

Q2 A light ray was shone from air into some water. The ray had an **angle of incidence** of **30°** and an **angle of refraction** of **22°**. Use this data to calculate the **refractive index** of water.

....

....

Q3 Optical fibres work because of repeated **total internal reflections**.

a) Complete the **ray diagrams** below. The critical angle for glass/air is **42°**.

You'll need to measure the angle of incidence for each one — carefully.

b) What two conditions are essential for **total internal reflection** to occur?

1. ....

2. ....

c) Describe an **experiment** to find the critical angle of a **glass/air boundary** using the **equipment pictured on the right**.

....

....

....

....

....

....

P3a Topic 1 — Radiation and Treatment

Uses of Total Internal Reflection

Q1 Choose from the words below to complete the passage.

| reflected | internal | diffraction | dense | core |

Optical fibres depend on total .... reflection for their operation.
Visible light is sent down the cable and is .... when it hits the boundary
between the .... of the fibre and the less .... outer case.

Q2 The diagrams show rays of light in an **optical fibre**.
Draw arrows to match each diagram to the correct description of what is happening.

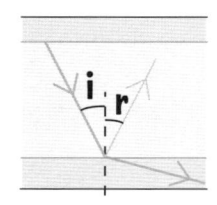

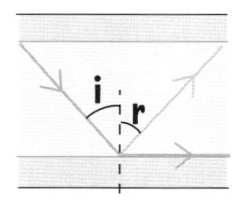

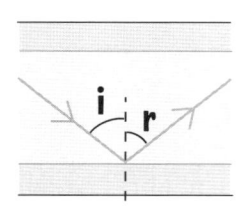

Total internal reflection

Most of the light passes out of the optical fibre, but some is reflected internally.

Most of the light is reflected internally, but some emerges along the surface of the glass.

Q3 What is meant by the 'critical angle' for a material?

....

....

Q4 Doctors use **endoscopes** to look inside patients' bodies. Endoscopes work using **optical fibres**.

a) What **material** could the optical fibres in an endoscope be made from?

....

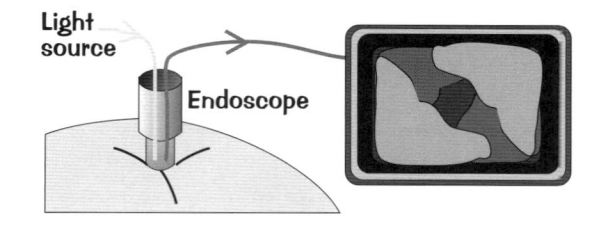

b) Explain why doctors try not to **bend** an endoscope sharply.

....

....

....

P3a Topic 1 — Radiation and Treatment

Uses of Total Internal Reflection

Q5 Light passes through the acrylic bottom of a boat into the water below. For blue light, the refractive index of **acrylic** is **1.498** (to 3 d.p.) and the refractive index of **water** is **1.337** (to 3 d.p.)

    a) i) What happens to the **speed** of the light as it passes into the water?

        ....

       ii) Complete this sentence by underlining the correct option.

          The angle of refraction is **greater than** / **less than** the angle of incidence.

    b) If the angle of incidence were equal to the critical angle, what would the **angle** of **refraction** be?

    ....

    c) What happens to light which enters the water at an angle **greater** than the critical angle?

    ....

    ....

    d) Calculate the **critical angle** for the **acrylic to water** boundary for blue light, to the nearest degree.

You'll need the equation with sin C in it.

    ....

    ....

    ....

Q6 The diagram shows the use of an **endoscope** in **keyhole surgery**.

    a) Explain what is meant by the term **keyhole surgery**.

    ....

    ....

    b) Outline how an **endoscope** works.

    ....

    ....

    c) List two **advantages** of keyhole surgery over conventional surgery.

      1. ....

      2. ....

P3a Topic 1 — Radiation and Treatment

Electron Beams

Q1 The **current** carried by a beam of electrons is **4 mA**.

a) What is current a measure of?

....

b) How many **electrons** pass a certain point in the beam per second?

....

....

For this question, use $q = 1.6 \times 10^{-19}$ C.

Q2 An **electron** accelerates across a potential difference (voltage) of 4 kV. The charge on the electron is -1.6×10^{-19} C.

a) Calculate the **kinetic energy** gained by the electron.

....

b) How much **potential energy** will the electron lose?

....

Think about energy conservation.

Q3 The diagram to the right shows a machine for taking **dental X-rays**.

a) The filament is heated so that it **emits** electrons. What is the name of this process?

....

b) Sketch in and label the **path of the electron beam** on the diagram. Show the direction of the beam.

c) Sketch in and label the **path of the X-rays** on the diagram. Show the direction of the beam.

d) Why does the **electron beam** move from cathode to the anode?

....

....

e) At the **anode** the electrons from the beam strike atoms of the metal, causing them to emit **X-rays**. Where does the energy for the X-rays come from?

....

f) The equipment is contained in an **evacuated** glass tube, surrounded by lead casing. Explain why the glass case is evacuated.

An evacuated tube means a tube that contains a vacuum.

....

....

X-ray Intensity and Absorption

Q1 Explain why X-rays are highly **ionising**, in terms of their **energy** and **frequency**.

....

....

....

Q2 After falling off his skateboard, Tony goes to hospital to see if any of the bones in his hand are broken. A radiographer takes an **X-ray** photograph of his hand.

a) Use the words below to fill in the blanks to explain why the radiographer stands far away from the X-ray machine during Tony's X-ray.

four   intensity   eight   inverse   three

> If the radiographer moves twice as far from the X-ray source, the same radiation from the source is spread over .... times the area.
> So the radiographer only receives $\frac{1}{2^2} = \frac{1}{4}$ of the intensity of the radiation.
> This relationship is known as the .... square law.

b) The X-ray tube used to produce the X-rays is contained within a **lead casing**.

The graph below shows how the **intensity** of the X-rays passing **through** the casing changes depending on the **thickness** of the lead.

Use the graph to describe the **relationship** between the **absorption** of the X-rays passing through the lead and its **thickness**.

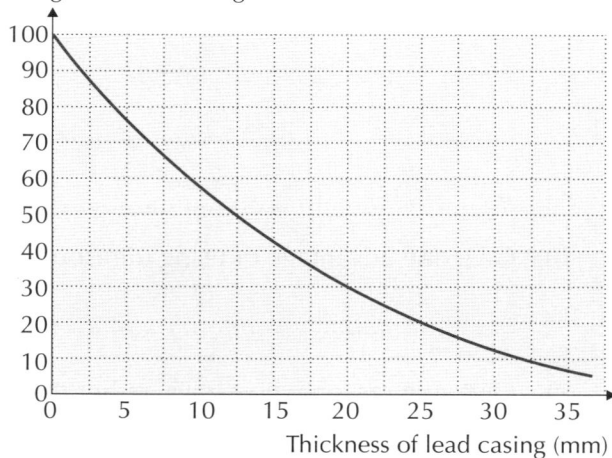

....

....

....

....

....

Top Tips:
These ideas all **link together** — X-rays are **highly ionising** because of their frequency and energy. So that means anyone using them has to keep their distance (except the patient). Usefully though, we can stick some materials between us and the X-rays to reduce our exposure to them. Phew.

P3a Topic 2 — X-rays and ECGs

X-ray Imaging

Q1 Tick the boxes to show whether each of these statements is **true** or **false**.

		True	False
a)	Gamma rays are used in computerised axial tomography (CAT) scans.	☐	☐
b)	CAT scans produce low resolution images.	☐	☐
c)	CAT scans can be used to treat tumours and cancers.	☐	☐
d)	CAT scans can be used to produce 3D images of the body.	☐	☐

Q2 Fluoroscopes use X-rays to create **moving images** of patients' insides.

Choose from the words given below to complete the passage about how **fluoroscopes** work.

| intensity | fluoresces | fluorescent | brighter | passed | between | recorded |

A patient is placed .... an X-ray source and a .... screen. The .... of X-rays reaching the screen depends on what they've .... through in the body. The X-rays hit the screen which absorbs them and .... (gives off light) to show a live image on a screen. The higher the intensity of the X-rays, the .... the screen. The screen is attached to a computer so the images can be ....

Q3 Both **X-rays** and **ultrasound** can be used to image the inside of the body.

a) Use the words below to help you briefly describe **how X-rays** are used in **CAT** scans.

beam   rotates   detectors   computer   absorbed   image

....
....
....
....

b) Give **one** advantage of using ultrasound over CAT scans.

....

c) Give **one** reason why X-rays, rather than ultrasound, might be used to create an image of a patient.

....

d) Suggest a reason why X-rays are often used to diagnose a patient's medical condition, even though they're potentially harmful.

....

P3a Topic 2 — X-rays and ECGs

Electricity and the Body

Q1 A machine can be used to detect small **electrical signals** in a patient's muscles. These results can be used to **identify** problems with the muscles.

    a) Define the following terms:

        i) resting potential ....

        ....

        ii) action potential ....

        ....

    b) What value would you expect to record from a **contracted** muscle cell in a healthy person?

    ....

Q2 Electrocardiographs are used to measure the activity of the **heart**.

    a) Describe, briefly, the **structure** of the heart.

    ....

    b) Describe how a series of electrical signals help to produce a heart beat.

    ....

    ....

    c) Describe the sensors used to detect the action potentials of a patient's heart.

    ....

Q3 The diagram below shows a typical **ECG** (electrocardiogram).

    a) Show the size of the **resting potential** with an arrow on the y-axis.

    b) What is the **period** of the heartbeat? ....

    c) Calculate the frequency of the heartbeat in **beats per minute.**

    ....

    d) What **muscle action** in the heart is being recorded at points:

        i) P ....

        ii) QRS ....

        iii) T ....

Top Tips: With a title like "Electricity and the Body", this page had so much potential. Chortle. Learn the shape of a normal ECG and know how all the different parts relate to the action of the heart.

P3a Topic 2 — X-rays and ECGs

Pace Makers and Pulse Oximeters

Q1 The diagram to the right shows a **pulse oximeter** on a hospital patient's **finger**.

a) Add arrows to the diagram to show the direction of the red light and infrared beams.

b) Choose from the words given below to complete the passage about how a pulse oximeter works.

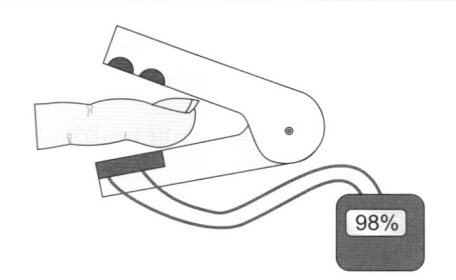

reflected	reduced	absorbed	calibrated	monkey	tissue	increased

Red and infrared light pass through the .... and are detected by a photo detector. Some of the light is .... by the red blood so that the amount of light detected by the detector is .... The amount of light absorbed depends on the amount of oxyhaemoglobin in the blood so the display can be .... to show the blood's oxyhaemoglobin content.

c) State one other suitable part of the **body** where a pulse oximeter could be placed. Explain your answer.

....

....

Q2 Arthur has been diagnosed with a **heart problem**. He is being fitted with an artificial **pacemaker** under the skin near his collarbone.

Briefly describe the function of a pacemaker and how it works.

....

....

....

Q3 **Reflection** pulse oximetry is used to measure the amount of oxygen in the blood.

a) How does reflection pulse oximetry differ from the type of pulse oximetry described in question **1**?

....

b) Connect the boxes below to complete the sentences about haemoglobin.

| Oxyhaemoglobin is... | ...purply coloured... | ...and doesn't contain much oxygen. |

| Reduced haemoglobin is... | ...bright red... | ...and rich in oxygen. |

P3a Topic 2 — X-rays and ECGs

Mixed Questions — P3a Topics 1 & 2

Q1 Karen has hurt her foot playing football. She is having an **X-ray** to find out whether she has broken a bone.

a) The X-rays have an **intensity** of 430 W/m². The surface area of Karen's foot is 0.024 m². Calculate the approximate **power** of the radiation reaching Karen's foot.

....

b) What does '**radiation**' mean?

....

c) Karen is given special glasses to wear while the X-ray is taken. Explain why.

....

....

d) The radiographer goes behind a lead screen while Karen has her X-ray. Why does he does this?

....

Q2 Nurse Horton uses a **pulse oximeter** to monitor the blood oxygen content of a patient who has recently had surgery.

a) Describe and explain how a pulse oximeter works.

....

....

....

b) If the blood has a high oxygen content, what colour will the oxyhaemoglobin appear?

....

Q3 **Ultrasound** is used in pre-natal scanning.

a) Briefly describe **how** ultrasound is used to form an image of a foetus.

....

....

b) Explain why ultrasound is used in pre-natal scanning rather than X-rays.

....

....

c) Give **two** other medical uses of ultrasound. ....

....

P3a Topic 2 — X-rays and ECGs

Mixed Questions — P3a Topics 1 & 2

Q4 James' doctor thinks he may have a cancerous tumour in his intestine. The surgeon decides to investigate further using **keyhole surgery**.

a) Name the **instrument** the surgeon would use to see inside James' body. ....

b) The instrument contains **optical fibres** to carry light into James' body and an image back out. Describe how light is carried along an optical fibre.

....

....

....

c) During the operation James is connected to an **ECG** machine to monitor the activity of his heart.

  i) What does an ECG measure?

  ....

  ii) Sketch the shape of a typical ECG on the axes provided. Label the components of the curve.

d) The time from peak to peak on James' ECG is **0.75 s**. Calculate the frequency of his heart beat.

....

Q5 Andrew and Cassie are looking at a shell. They can see it because images **form on their retinas**.

a) Complete the paths of the light rays on the diagram below for an eye with normal sight.

b) The light entering Cassie's eye is shown in the diagram to the right. Her lens is working correctly.

Circle the correct words to complete the sentences below.

Cassie's eyeball is too long / short, so images form behind / in front of her retina.

This can be corrected by diverging / converging spectacle lenses which make light rays come together.

c) Andrew uses a **magnifying glass** to examine the shell. He finds that to see a magnified image of the shell, the right way up, he must hold the lens less than 3 cm from it.

What is the focal length of this lens? ....

P3a Topic 2 — X-rays and ECGs

Mixed Questions — P3a Topics 1 & 2

Q6 Deirdre is long-sighted. She wears glasses to correct her vision.

a) The lens for her right eye has a focal length of **0.4 m**.

  i) Calculate the **power** of the lens.

  ....

  ....

  ii) The lens for her left eye is made of the **same material** as the lens for her right eye, but has a **higher power**. Describe how the two lenses will differ in appearance.

  ....

b) Deirdre is considering undergoing **laser eye** surgery to **correct** her vision.

  i) Give **one** possible risk associated with laser correction.

  ....

  ii) Suggest **one** other way she could correct her sight.

  ....

Q7 The diagram below shows an **X-ray tube**.

a) Name and describe the process by which the filament releases electrons into the X-ray tube.

  ....

  ....

b) Each electron released is accelerated by a potential difference of 55 kV. Calculate the kinetic energy gained by each electron.

Use charge on an electron = 1.6×10^{-19}.

  ....

  ....

c) X-rays used in **fluoroscopy** are produced using X-ray tubes.

  The patient is placed between the X-ray tube and a fluorescent screen.
  Briefly describe how the **fluorescent screen** is used to produce a live **image** of inside the body.

  ....

  ....

  ....

  ....

P3a Topic 2 — X-rays and ECGs

Particles in Atoms

Q1 Alpha, beta and gamma are all types of ionising radiation, but they have quite different properties.

a) Rate the different types of radiation according to their penetrating power.

1 = high penetrating power
2 = moderate penetrating power
3 = low penetrating power

alpha ☐   beta ☐   gamma ☐

b) How does the **penetrating power** of each type of radiation compare to its **ionising power**?

....

c) Give an example of a material that can stop

　i) **alpha** radiation ....   ii) **beta** radiation ....

Q2 Indicate whether the following statements are **true** or **false**.

　　　　　　　　　　　　　　　　　　　　　　　　　　　　　　　　True False

a) A positron is a positively charged neutron. ☐ ☐

b) The number of protons in an atom are equal to the number of electrons. ☐ ☐

c) Positrons, electrons and neutrons all have the same relative mass. ☐ ☐

d) The relative charge on a proton is +1. ☐ ☐

e) Positrons have the same ionising and penetration properties as an electron. ☐ ☐

Q3 Neutrons are found in the nuclei of atoms and can also be emitted as a form of radiation. Underline the correct words from the options given.

a) Neutron radiation is **more** / **less** penetrating than alpha or beta radiation.

b) Neutrons do not have electric **charge** / **power** so they do not directly **absorb** / **ionise** material they pass through.

c) Absorbing a neutron can make a nucleus **ionised** / **radioactive**.

Q4 Shielding made of **concrete** can be used as protection against neutron radiation.

a) Explain how the shielding works.

....

b) Concrete shielding alone is not enough to prevent the harmful effects of neutron radiation. Explain why.

....

....

c) Write down an example of a material that could be added to the shielding to stop any radiation getting through. ....

Stability and Radioactive Decay

Q1 Complete each of the sentences about **radioactive decay** by choosing the correct words or numbers from the list below each one. You may use some words more than once.

a) During α decay, the nucleus loses .... protons and .... neutrons.

So its nucleon number decreases by .... and its proton number decreases by ....

       1   **2**   **3**   **4**

b) During β⁻ decay a .... becomes a .... The proton number increases by 1 and the nucleon number ....

    stays the same   **proton**   **neutron**   **electron**   **increases**

c) During β⁺ decay a .... becomes a .... The proton number .... and the nucleon number stays the same.

    proton   **increases by 1**   **stays the same**   **neutron**   **decreases by 1**

d) α, β⁺ or β⁻ decay results in the formation of a different ...., which is shown by the change in .... number.

    element   **nucleon**   **proton**

e) When a nucleus emits a γ ray, its mass number changes by .... and its proton number changes by ....

       0   **1**   **2**   **4**

Q2 The equation shows an isotope of carbon undergoing radioactive decay.

$$^{14}_{6}C \rightarrow X + ^{0}_{+1}e$$

a) What type of radioactive decay is this?

....

b) Give the **nucleon number** and **proton number** of element X.

nucleon number: ....

proton number: ....

c) People take precautions against cell damage from ionisation by most types of radiation. Why is it not necessary to take particular precautions against this type of radiation?

....

Top Tips: A β⁺ decay here, a β⁻ decay there. This all might seem a tad confusing, but it's important to get your head around what becomes what, e.g. a neutron turning into a proton etc. Make sure you know how the proton and nucleon numbers are affected by α, β⁺ or β⁻ decay too.

P3b Topic 3 — Radioactivity and Ionising Radiation

Stability and Radioactive Decay

Q3 The graph on the right shows the number of neutrons (N) against the number of protons (Z) for **stable isotopes**.

a) What are **isotopes** of an element?

....

....

b) Are isotopes in region A stable or unstable? Circle your answer.

    stable   unstable

c) Are isotopes in region A neutron-rich or proton-rich?

    neutron-rich   proton-rich

d) Suggest a reason why isotopes in region B are **unstable**.

....

e) In order to achieve stability, what type of decay will isotopes in **region B** undergo?

....

f) What type of decay will isotopes in **region C** undergo in order to achieve stability?

....

g) What type of particle will isotopes in **region D** emit in order to become more stable?

....

Q4 **Alpha particles** are strongly ionising.

a) What kinds of atom undergo alpha decay?

....

b) Circle the two of these elements that undergo alpha decay.

    H   U   Th   C   He

c) Complete this nuclear equation.

$$^{224}_{88}Ra \rightarrow \boxed{}Rn + \boxed{}\text{alpha}$$

d) After alpha (or beta) decay, a nucleus often has too much energy. How does it lose this energy?

....

P3b Topic 3 — Radioactivity and Ionising Radiation

Quarks

Q1 Tick the statements that are **true**.

a) Quarks are made up of protons and neutrons. ☐

b) The relative mass of a quark is 1/3. ☐

c) All quarks have the same charge. ☐

d) There are 2 quarks in a proton. ☐

e) There are 2 types of quark in a neutron. ☐

Q2 Match the **particles** on the left with the correct description of their properties.

Down-quark — relative mass 1/3, relative charge +2/3

Proton — relative mass 1, charge +1

Neutron — relative charge –1/3

Up-quark — made up of two down-quarks and one up-quark

Q3 The number of protons and neutrons in a nucleus can make it **unstable**.

a) Complete the following sentence.

To become more stable, the nucleus can convert a neutron into a ....

b) What particle must be emitted to keep the overall charge zero? ....

c) What is this process called? ....

Q4 The **charges** on protons and neutrons are determined by the **quarks** that form them.

a) Make simple sketch diagrams of a **proton** and a **neutron**, showing the number and type of quarks each contains.

Proton	Neutron

b) Complete the blanks in this sentence:

In β⁺ decay, a proton is converted to a .... and a .... is emitted.

c) Describe β⁺ decay in terms of what happens to the quarks in a proton.

....

P3b Topic 3 — Radioactivity and Ionising Radiation

Medical Uses of Radiation

Q1 **Positron emission tomography** (PET) is a scanning technique used in hospitals.

    a) Give one advantage and one disadvantage of PET compared to X-rays.

        i) advantage: ....

        ii) disadvantage: ....

    b) Give two conditions that can be diagnosed using PET.

....

Q2 Put the following stages in the right order to explain how PET is carried out.

    ☐ The tracer moves through the body to the organs.

    ☐ Detectors around the body record the position of the emitted gamma rays.

    ☐ The patient is injected with the tracer.

    ☐ The positrons collide with electrons and are annihilated, releasing gamma rays.

    ☐ The radioisotope emits positrons.

    [1] A positron-emitting radioactive isotope is added to a substance used by the body to make a tracer.

    ☐ A computer builds up a map of radioactivity in the body.

Q3 The **map of radioactivity** in the body produced by a PET scan can be used to detect active cancer tumours.

    a) **i)** What does the map of radioactivity match up with?

....

        ii) Why is this?

....

    b) Explain why a PET scan is a good way to detect cancer.

....

    c) Why is PET not used frequently on the same patient?

....

Q4 **Radiation exposure** can be damaging, but is also used as a medical treatment.

    a) Explain how radiotherapy can be used as a form of **palliative care**.

....

....

    b) Describe **two** ways that radiation can damage cells.

....

P3b Topic 3 — Radioactivity and Ionising Radiation

Medical Uses of Radiation

Q5 A hospital has recently installed a new PET scanner and a cyclotron to produce the isotopes needed.

a) Explain why the isotopes used in PET scanners have to be produced nearby.

....

....

b) The medical personnel using the equipment must take precautions to limit their exposure to ionising radiation. Write down **two** precautions they could take to minimise their exposure.

1. ....

2. ....

Q6 Radiation can be used **internally** and **externally** to treat tumours.

a) What is internal radiation therapy?

....

b) Give **one** advantage of internal radiation therapy over the use of external sources of radiation.

....

c) Describe **one** advantage of using external treatments instead of internal radiation therapy.

....

....

Q7 Imagine a **new** technique using **radiation** has been developed to treat breast cancer. It has been tested on people with end-stage breast cancer, and shown to be an effective treatment with tolerable side effects.

a) The technique has not been tested on people with early-stage breast cancer.

i) Why might someone with early-stage breast cancer want to receive treatment using this new technique?

....

ii) Suggest why doctors would be unwilling to give this new treatment to patients with early-stage breast cancer.

....

b) There are many **ethical** issues associated with the use of radiotherapy. Outline one such issue.

....

....

P3b Topic 3 — Radioactivity and Ionising Radiation

Cyclotrons

Q1 A **satellite** orbiting the Earth travels at a constant speed.

a) Is the satellite accelerating? Explain your answer.

....

b) Put a tick next to each true statement below.

☐ "If a body is accelerating then there must be a resultant force acting on it."

☐ "The forces acting on a body going round in a circle at a steady speed must be balanced."

☐ "If there is no resultant force acting on a body then it carries on moving in a straight line at the same speed."

c) What is the general name for a force that keeps a body moving in a circular path?

....

Q2 Choose from the words given below to complete the passage.

curved	magnetic	spirals	lose	perpendicular

A charged particle in a .... field will experience a force. The force is always .... to its direction of travel — so the particle follows a .... path. If only a magnetic field is present, the particles will move in .... rather than circles because they .... energy and slow down as they interact with other particles.

Q3 A cyclotron is a type of **particle accelerator**. The diagram to the right shows the path of a charged particle in a cyclotron.

The charged particle starts at the centre of the cyclotron.

a) Describe the path of the particle as it moves through the cyclotron.

....

b) Explain why the particle follows the path described in part a).

....

....

....

....

Think about the energy of the particles and what the magnetic field is used for.

Uses of Particle Accelerators

Q1 Bombarding stable elements with **protons** can produce **radioactive isotopes**. Complete the following passage using some of the words provided.

nucleus	accelerator	cyclotron	electron	proton	element	mass

A proton is absorbed by the .... This increases its

.... number so a new .... is produced.

The proton needs a lot of energy before it can be absorbed by the nucleus, so this process

takes place in a particle .... called a ....

Q2 The radioactive isotopes produced by proton bombardment are **unstable**.

a) Complete the following equations to show how two radioactive isotopes are formed.

$$^{18}_{8}O + ^{1}_{1}p \longrightarrow ^{\square}_{\square}F + ^{1}_{0}n \qquad ^{14}_{7}N + ^{1}_{1}p \longrightarrow ^{\square}_{\square}C + ^{4}_{2}He$$

b) i) What sort of radiation do the radioactive isotopes formed in this way usually emit?

....

ii) Suggest a medical use for these radioactive isotopes.

....

Q3 Scientists at CERN use an enormous **particle accelerator** to smash particles into each other at tremendous speeds.

a) Explain how particle accelerators can help scientists gain a better understanding about the Universe.

....

....

....

b) Give two reasons why scientists from all over Europe collaborate on the research at CERN.

....

....

....

....

Alan and the guys hadn't realised collaborative working meant one computer between five.

Top Tips: Proton bombardment — that sounds pretty scary. But it's actually really useful. Cyclotrons are used to bombard protons at stable isotopes to create radioactive isotopes for use in medicine. Oh Mr Proton Bombardment, you're not so scary after all. I'm sorry I ever doubted you.

P3b Topic 4 — Motion of Particles

Momentum and Kinetic Energy

Q1 The diagram shows a fast moving **neutron colliding** with a stationary sodium **nucleus** and bouncing off again.

a) Using the notation in the diagram, write an expression for:

i) the total momentum before the collision.

....

ii) the total momentum after the collision.

....

b) Using your answers to part **a)**, explain what is meant by the term **conservation of momentum**.

....

Q2 The diagram shows the **alpha decay** of **uranium-238**.

Use the relative masses in your calculations.

a) i) Add an arrow to the box on the diagram to show which way the **thorium** nucleus will move.

ii) Explain why it must move this way.

....
....

b) Calculate the **velocity** of the thorium nucleus immediately after the decay.

....

Q3 Tick the boxes to show the properties **conserved** in an:

	KE	Momentum
a) elastic collision.	☐	☐
b) inelastic collision.	☐	☐

Strawberry = conserved.

Q4 A 1 kg ball moving at a velocity of 4 m/s collides with a stationary ball of mass of 3 kg. After the collision, both balls move off in opposite directions.

a) Calculate the total kinetic energy before the collision.

....
....

b) Was kinetic energy conserved in the collision? Show your working.

....
....

P3b Topic 4 — Motion of Particles

Momentum and Kinetic Energy

Q5 The diagram below shows the **collision** of a neutron and an atom of uranium-235.

$^{1}_{0}n$ $^{235}_{92}U$

v = 2 km/s   v = 0.1 km/s

a) Calculate the relative momentum of the:

i) neutron. ....

ii) uranium-235 nucleus. ....

b) The uranium-235 nucleus absorbs the neutron to form uranium-236.

i) What is the relative momentum of the uranium-236 isotope?

....

ii) Calculate the velocity of the uranium-236 isotope.

....

c) Was the collision elastic or inelastic? Show your working.

....

....

....

Q6 Kobe is testing two bouncy balls. He wants to find out which ball is the bounciest. He drops both balls from a height of **100 cm** onto a wooden floor. He records their rebound heights for three subsequent bounces. His results are shown in the table below.

a) Name the type of energy the balls have just before they're dropped.

....

b) Which ball was the bounciest?

....

	Ball 1	Ball 2
Height of 1st bounce (cm)	63	76
Height of 2nd bounce (cm)	45	55
Height of 3rd bounce (cm)	22	31

c) Explain why the balls never reach the same height as their previous bounce.

....

....

d) Suggest **one** factor Kobe could change to alter the rebound heights of the balls.

....

Top Tips:
If you know your equations, this topic is the chance to earn some tasty marks without too much trouble. Learning equations isn't the most exciting job in the world — but it does pay off. Remember, things with momentum are **moving** — and that momentum equation — m × v.

P3b Topic 4 — Motion of Particles

Annihilation and PET Scans

Q1 The diagram represents the **collision** of an **electron** and a **positron**.

a) What happens when a particle collides with its antiparticle?
....

b) The electron and positron are travelling at the same speed before the collision. What is the value of their **total momentum** immediately before the collision?
....

c) Choose the correct words from each pair to complete the sentences below.

The collision of an electron and a positron produces a pair of **gamma rays** / **radioactive particles**. The **gamma rays** / **radioactive particles** produced have the same **energy** / **velocity** as each other, and opposite **energies** / **velocities**.

d) What is the value of the **total momentum** immediately after the collision? Explain your answer.
....

e) Read the statement below.

"Charge isn't conserved in a positron and electron annihilation, because the total charge after is zero."

Do you agree with the statement? Explain your answer.
....
....

f) Explain how this collision is an example of mass energy conservation.
....

g) Calculate the minimum energy released when an electron and positron collide. The mass of an electron/positron is 9.1×10^{-31} kg and the speed of light is 3×10^8 m/s.
....
....

Q2 Below is a diagram showing a patient undergoing a **PET scan**. Before the scan, the patient was injected with a **positron-emitting radio isotope**.

Use the diagram to help you explain how the radio isotope is used in PET scanning.
....
....
....
....

P3b Topic 4 — Motion of Particles

Kinetic Theory and Absolute Zero

Q1 Tick the correct boxes below to show whether the sentences are true or false.

		True	False
a)	The particles in a **liquid** are free to move at **high** speeds.	☐	☐
b)	The particles in a gas have **more** energy than those in liquids and solids.	☐	☐
c)	In a solid, the particles can only **vibrate** about a fixed position.	☐	☐
d)	In a liquid, the particles form **irregular** arrangements.	☐	☐
e)	The particles in a liquid have **less** energy than those in a solid.	☐	☐

Q2 Complete the following paragraph by choosing words from the box below.

0 °C	ice	0 K	100 °C	−273 °C	absolute	water

The Celsius temperature scale has two fixed points. One is the melting point of .... at .... The other is the boiling point of .... at .... The lowest fixed point on the Kelvin temperature scale is at the lowest temperature possible — called .... zero. This is given a value of .... and it is equivalent to a temperature on the Celsius scale of about ....

Q3 Convert the following temperatures to **kelvin** (K).

a) 3 °C .... b) 210 °C ....

c) −45 °C .... d) 0 °C ....

Q4 Convert the following temperatures to **°C**.

a) 0 K .... b) 300 K ....

c) 640 K .... d) 30 K ....

Q5 Explain, in terms of the **movement of particles**, why there is a theoretical absolute zero temperature.

....

....

....

Pressure, Volume and Temperature of Gases

Q1 Complete the following sentences by choosing the correct word(s) from each pair.

   a) When a gas is heated, the particles in it move **faster** / **more slowly**.

   b) The average **kinetic** / **potential** energy of particles in a gas is **equal** / **proportional** to the temperature of the gas on the kelvin scale.

   c) For a gas at a constant pressure, the volume is **proportional** / **inversely proportional** to temperature.

Q2 **Kinetic theory** can be used to explain the behaviour and properties of gases.

   a) What does kinetic theory say that a gas consists of? Circle **two** of the options A to E below.

        A stationary particles   B very small particles   C a rigid mesh of particles

        D mostly empty space   E fluctuations in electric and magnetic fields

   b) Explain how the impact of gas molecules on the sides of a container relates to the pressure of a gas.

        ....

        ....

Q3 The kinetic energy of particles depends on their **mass** and their **velocity**.

   a) What is the **formula** for the kinetic energy of a particle of mass **m** travelling at velocity **v**?

        ....

   b) The temperature of a gas is increased from 277 °C to 827 °C. At 277 °C the mean kinetic energy of the gas is 1.14×10^{20} joules. What is it at 827 °C?

Always start a kinetic theory question involving temperature by converting degrees Celsius to kelvin.

        ....

        ....

   c) Explain why it takes longer for the smell of air freshener to spread through a room on a cold day than on a hot day.

        ....

Q4 A bag of elephant trump is kept in a sealed bag at **300 K**. The bag is carelessly left on a radiator. The gas heats up to a temperature of **345 K** and the volume expands to **0.575 m³**. Calculate the initial volume of the gas if the pressure remains constant.

        ....

        ....

        ....

        ....

P3b Topic 5 — Kinetic Theory and Gases

Pressure, Volume and Temperature of Gases

Q5 Ruth is using a **gas syringe** to investigate **ideal gas laws**. In her first experiment, she investigates the relationship between **volume** and **temperature**.

a) Use words from the box to complete the description of the experiment below. You may not need some of the words.

outwards	expand	inwards	air	contracts
increases	volume	Bunsen burner	pressure	

The gas syringe is half filled with .... and sealed with a rubber bung.

The syringe plunger is free to move, allowing the gas to be kept at a constant

.... A .... is used to heat the gas, causing it to

.... The syringe plunger is observed to move ....

as the gas is heated. When the gas cools back down again, the plunger moves

back to its original position because the gas .... as it cools.

This shows volume .... as temperature of the gas increases.

b) Describe an experiment Ruth could do using a pressure sensor with the gas syringe to investigate the relationship between pressure and volume. Say what this experiment would show.

....

....

....

....

Q6 The gas in the container on the right has an initial volume of **0.65 m³** and an initial pressure of **101 325 Pa**.

a) Calculate the pressure of the gas if the volume is reduced to **0.45 m³** and the temperature remains constant

....

....

b) Explain, in terms of **particle collisions**, the reason for the change in pressure you calculated in part **a)**.

....

....

....

P3b Topic 5 — Kinetic Theory and Gases

Gas Pressure and Medicine

Q1 A bubble of carbon dioxide leaves a plant at the bottom of a lake. Initially it has a volume of **5 cm³** and is at a pressure of **607 950 Pa**. The temperature at the bottom of the lake is **4 °C**. The bubble rises and just before it reaches the surface it is at a pressure of **101 325 Pa** and a temperature of **20 °C**.

    a) Give two reasons why the volume of the bubble will **increase** as it rises.

        1. ....

        2. ....

    b) Calculate the **volume** of the bubble just before it reaches the surface.

Don't forget to convert temperatures to kelvin.

Q2 Gases are often used in **hospitals**, where they have to be kept in **pressurised canisters**.

    a) Give **two** reasons why hospitals store gases in canisters at pressures higher than atmospheric pressure.

        1. ....

        2. ....

    b) A **1750 cm³** canister stores nitrogen gas at a temperature of **300 K** and a pressure of **8 atm**. The pressure outside the canister is **1 atm** and the temperature is **300 K**.

Remember that pressure can be measured in Pa or atm. If both the initial and final pressures are in atm, there's no need to convert to Pa.

        i) What is the maximum volume of nitrogen that can be released from the canister?

        ii) The canister is fitted with a valve that controls its flow rate. Calculate how long it will take the canister to release the volume of gas you calculated in part **b) i)**, in minutes, if the flow rate is **5 cm³** per second.

Top Tips: Don't let questions with lots of different values phase you — it's really just a matter of figuring out which equation to use and plugging in the numbers. In gas canister questions, remember that the canister will never empty completely — the gas stops flowing when the pressures inside and outside the canister are equal, so some gas will always be left behind.

P3b Topic 5 — Kinetic Theory and Gases

Mixed Questions — P3b Topics 3, 4 & 5

Q1 When **high-energy** electrons are fired at protons and neutrons the deflection of the electrons shows that both protons and neutrons are made up of charged particles called **quarks**.

a) Describe the relative charge and mass of these types of quark, found in protons and neutrons.

  i) up-quarks: ....

  ii) down-quarks: ....

b) Write down the quark configuration of a proton.

  ....

Q2 Anna is investigating the properties of stable and unstable isotopes. She fires neutrons at a stable isotope of carbon. The isotope **absorbs a neutron** and becomes unstable. Anna adds the unstable isotope to a graph showing the number of neutrons against the number of protons in stable isotopes.

a) Would you expect the unstable carbon isotope to lie above, below or on the line of stability on the graph? Give a reason for your answer.

  ....

b) i) Complete the following equation describing the decay of the isotope: $^{13}_{6}C \longrightarrow {}^{\square}_{\square}N + {}^{0}_{-1}e$

  ii) What is this sort of decay called? ....

c) Describe the decay in terms of what happens to the **quarks** in a neutron within the isotope's nucleus.

  ....

d) The isotope is still unstable because it has too much **energy**. How can the isotope become stable?

  ....

Q3 A container of ideal gas has a pressure of 1×10^5 **Pa** and a volume of **100 cm³**.

a) The volume of the gas is gradually increased while the temperature remains constant. Calculate the **pressure** of the gas at the following volumes.

  i) 200 cm³ ....

  ii) 400 cm³ ....

b) When the pressure of the gas is 1.25×10^4 Pa, what will its **volume** be?

  ....

  ....

c) On the grid opposite, draw a **graph** showing how pressure varies against volume at constant temperature for this gas.

P3b Topic 5 — Kinetic Theory and Gases

Mixed Questions — P3b Topics 3, 4 & 5

Q4 An atom of nitrogen is bombarded with **proton radiation** in a cyclotron.

a) Why does this process need to take place in a cyclotron?

....

b) The nitrogen nucleus absorbs a proton. Why does this result in a new **element**?

....

c) The new element formed is an unstable isotope of carbon. What sort of radiation would you expect it to emit?

....

Q5 One of Dr McLeod's patients has cancer and is being treated with **radiotherapy**.

a) What sort of radiation would be used in this treatment?

....

b) Dr McLeod thinks that the radiotherapy won't cure his patient's cancer, but will reduce her suffering. What type of care is this? ....

c) Dr McLeod hears about a new drug that might help his patient. The drug has not yet been tested on cancer patients and the company is looking for volunteers to take part in a trial. Outline an argument for and against this patient taking part in the trial.

For: ....

....

Against: ....

....

Q6 A **hydrogen atom** travels at a velocity of **300 m/s** when it collides elastically with a helium atom travelling in the **opposite direction** at a velocity of **−200 m/s**.

a) What **two** properties are conserved in an elastic collision?

....

b) The hydrogen atom leaves the collision with a **final velocity** of **−400 m/s**. Calculate the **final velocity** of the helium atom.

You'll need to use the relative atomic masses for helium and hydrogen.

....

....

....

P3b Topic 5 — Kinetic Theory and Gases